DELIVERED

FROM THE

TORMENT

A CHRISTIAN PERSPECTIVE ON SCHIZOPHRENIA

◆

LOU ANNE METCALFE

PublishAmerica
Baltimore

First printing

This publication contains the opinions and ideas of its author. Author intends to offer information of a general nature. Neither the author nor the publisher are engaged in rendering medical, health or any other kind of personal professional services to the reader. The reader should consult his or her own physician before relying on any information set forth in or implied from this publication. Any reliance on the information herein is at the reader's own discretion.

The author and publisher specifically disclaim all responsibility for any liability, loss, or right, personal or otherwise, which is incurred as a consequence, directly or indirectly, of the use and application of any contents of this book. They further make no representations or warranties with respect to the accuracy or completeness of the contents of this work and specifically disclaim all warranties including without limitation any implied warranty of fitness for a particular purpose. Any recommendations are made without any guarantee on the part of the author or the publisher.

PublishAmerica has allowed this work to remain exactly as the author intended, verbatim, without editorial input.

Hardcover 978-1-4489-3390-7
Softcover 978-1-4489-3391-4
PUBLISHED BY PUBLISHAMERICA, LLLP
www.publishamerica.com
Baltimore

Printed in the United States of America

DEDICATION

THIS BOOK IS DEDICATED FIRST AND FOREMOST TO ALMIGHTY YAWEH, MY GRANDMOTHER, MARY LOUISE STARK, MY AWESOME MOTHER AND DR. ABRAM HOFFER.

TABLE OF CONTENTS

FOREWORD

BY DR. ABRAM HOFFER, ORTHOMOLECULAR
PSYCHIATRIST, WORLD RENOWNED

During July 1977 about a year after I had opened my practice in Victoria B.C. Louanne came to see me with her mother, Margaret Anne Metcalfe.

Lou Anne then only thirteen years old was not well. She was irritable and sometimes behaved inappropriately, suffering from perceptual changes and was depressed.

Eventually she was diagnosed "Schizophrenic" which is a term I now abhor because it is so wrong. It tells us nothing about "CAUSE" and treatment and carries a lot of stigma with it. It is really a variant of pellagra; the Vitamin B-3 deficiency disease which at one time in the United States occupied one third of mental hospital beds in Southern United States.

It was indistinguishable from schizophrenia except that it was caused by a deficient diet. Mainly of corn, little meat and vegetables. This was a "killing disease" causing major skin changes, difficulty with digestion, mental changes and if not treated DEATH.

Modern schizophrenia is not due to just deficiency but the condition is a DEPENDENCY caused by an increased need for nourishment and for NIACIN, due to a defect in the "Niacin" receptors in the brain.

Lou Anne was immediately started on orthomolecular treatment which means that she was advised to follow a very good diet, taking vitamin supplements including niacin and vitamn C. She responded quickly \ul \ulnone before she reached her present state. \par

She needed to take small doses of some of the older tranquilizers and she had to be admitted for special treatment several times.

Eventually she suffered more severe changes such as voices and visions, but she was able to deal with them with admirable courage. She recovered and has become a productive member of society.

Had she been treated with DRUGS ONLY, I have no idea what she would be doing but she certainly would not have written THIS BOOK.

Louanne is a VERY GIFTED individual as are so many others with this condition. They have really good "genes" but neither her doctors or she and her mother were aware that even good genes have to be fed properly. In this case it means giving them the right vitamins and the correct doses. It is a pity that most patients who develop this condition are denied the chance for recovery through the \ul \ulnone RESISTANCE AND IGNORANCE OF THE PSYCHIATRIC ESTABLISHMENT.

— A. Hoffer PhD, MD FRCR (c)RMCP.

INTRODUCTION

I'll take you the reader on a journey that if I may say so will be electrifying, tearful, and above all to give HOPE to the devastating affects of schizophrenia. A most misunderstood illness afflicting the most "Gifted." The unappreciated GEMS of society.

They all say it's incurable. Really? I suppose then that I defy the odds.

This is my story, a slow EXODUS from Hell...

"Madness, provided it comes as the gift of Heaven is the channel by which we receive the greatest blessings...the men of old who gave things their names saw no disgrace or reproach in madness; otherwise they would not have connected it with the name of the noblest of all arts, the art of discerning the future, and called it the manic art... So, according to the evidence provided by our ancestors, madness is a nobler thing than sober sense... madness comes from God, whereas sober sense is merely human."

Socrates in his speech on divine madness in Phaedrus.

DREAMLAND BETWEEN TWO WORLDS

Signals dispersed in veils?
Foggy Images?
Fairytales?

Nightmarish shadows
Showing where the wind blows...
Warning that The Battle
Is On The Inside Of Your Windows...

One small family
One child sees the nightmare
Each night her pillow seems it is a
STONE..
Hesitant to fall asleep
To Hear the spirits moan...

Telling us direction
Revealing what's transpiring

Is it all nonsensical
To awake and be perspiring?

As The Battle rages
The predestined pages turn...
Now for clouds
Not to burn!

The Mare is not a horse
But there surely is a night..
No there isn't a so called Boogey-man

But the Opposer Of the Light

Looking back now it certainly makes sense
No option to be sitting on "The Fence."

Signals dispersed in veils?
Foggy Images.

Fairytales?

CHAPTER 1

I was born in Winnipeg, Manitoba on June 6th 1964.

My parents were divorced before I was born, which didn't bother me at all since I never knew any difference. Mark my brother, on the other hand was the one to manifest his turmoil and anger.

Manifest his inner disturbance concerning our father.

We came to Vancouver, B.C. after my grandfather died, I was only five years old. We lived in Richmond for just over a year.

Then we came to Victoria, when I was six, where I lived the majority of my young life.

My heritage is of a "Celtic Sword" and a Viking Helmet. Scottish, Swedish and a drop of a temper... Irish!!

Most obviously I take on the look of a swede with my blonde hair, height and build.

My grandfather Philip John Stark, had now been deceased not quite two years. A loss my grandmother never allowed to be subdued. We were the victims of her frustrated frenzy of grief. She was a cauldron of boiling pain, in denial towards the removal of an idolized soul mate.

Reckoned with later by God. I've come to understand her

intense grief as I now have a more enlightenened view on her plight. \par

Even at the tender age of three my grandfather was extremely special to me. He was a very kind, noble and profound human being. I knew he really loved me. I sensed his chosen soul. My knowing of him was so brief as he was only sixty-three when he passed away. Yet he left a profound mark on me. For all of my life to this very day.

CHAPTER 2

Of course the time for starting school is six years of age. I remember my teachers name was Miss Curry, who wore her hair in a beehive style. We were coming out of the late 60's The academics then were professional and intense. This was normal for us since we knew no different. School was always till at least 3:00 everyday sometimes till 4:00. The weather in Victoria, was mild similiar to some tropical places. To see snow near Christmas, was a rare occurence, and meeted with great joy, and activities corresponding. I'll always remember one of my happiest memories, when we lived on McRae Avenus. A thick snow fort was made by Mark, and a weekend, onwards with a couple of his friends entailed WW.3! Ducking behind the fort, running around to attack the other team, and in the inside of the snow fort, was a carefully dug cubby hole that housed quite a few very hard snowballs of ammunition. I thought this was a brilliant idea of my brother's, he had me of course making these sphere like weapons, in factory like precision. Then when it all melted away we were back to the Bahamas. This was something my mother and grandmother were desiring by leaving Winnipeg, the incredibly cold temperature. The sea, was another drawing factor for my grandmother. So we ended up living on an island surrounded literally by water.

I loved school intensely. I had a quiet demeanour and a good, quiet spirit. My little self drifted into that world of dreams, music and homework.

On our street Jasper Place, there were the three Walker girls. They instinctively knew my creative abilities and asked me to perform for them.

So I was the living T.V. screen and became Phil Donahue and Johnny Carson between two trees!

I didn't know till years later from my grandmother that this fact being among other things that I was being insidiously "mocked." Oh well, the many good things our innocent minds aren't even aware of.

My brother Mark and I were well—behaved children; quiet, playing in a civilized manner with our toys. Some people may not believe the way we were or how gentle I was. The Walker girls found it amusing to toss my long pom-pom hat, making me into the little piglet in the middle. The hat, the sweaters with the "ring" zippers. I think fondly of the 70's styles. Especially striking when your skinny.

I suppose there is much to say when you're six; the first grade, learning to ride a bike, or musical fascination. A big one for me.

One thing that is important for me to state here is that if it wasn't for my individuality and loner ability I wouldn't have survived. Yet we loners and suffering artists are victorious! Aren't we? If anyone on the planet is we are. I believe this with all my convictions.

At seven, I began my destiny with the piano.

My lessons were from the best teachers in Victoria. Classical, detailed, requiring hours of my own time in disciplined practice. I started to really compose at seven and eight years of age. Earning a place in the Times Colonist for a composition award. I also received a pen set with my name inscribed on it in gold lettering. I was a very sensitive child. It's great as far as creativity goes and hearing from God. Detrimental though in other respects. So from six yrs old until fourteen (When I was really ill.)I took piano lessons. I did extremely well. I received two First Class Honours and one Honours before the age of ten. I seemed to be naturally gifted with an ability at automatic memorization. Yet sight reading I found most difficult. Apparently I had a teacher who claimed that I had a "Fine" pianist's touch. I heard the other students smash out their Mozart, Bach etc. it was with a particular technical stamp.

The legitimate feeling I have for the music and respect for the instrument is a whole other factor.

At nine years of age I had my "debut" experience in a private school, St. Margaret's. I wore a beautiful red and green uniform with a tie the usual leotards and oxfords. We played grass hockey as the leading academic sport. I found the grass hockey sticks rather low, since I was the tallest girls in my grade. This was more of a big deal back then. Not an issue these days for teenagers to be 5' 9" and over.

I continued my piano lessons at the boarding school. Sometimes my mother would not be there to pick me up till after 6:00 p.m. She was doing the special counsellor thing. So I would watch the T.V. there in the lounge. I enjoyed this.

CHAPTER 3

Throughout the week particularily on the weekends my grandmother would often hear a variety of voices in friendly interaction under our deck stairs. She thought, what little friends has Lou Anne invited over? She was rather stunned to see it was just me. I was Alice in my own "Wonderland." I would conduct whole puppet shows; three puppets simultaneously if I could master it. I designed the shows poster, tickets putting the poster on my bedroom door. It didn't seem to register or faze on my little person that the audience consisted of only two people! My grandmother and my mother!

Also prepared in my bedroom theatre were my dolls, each one unique and high quality. Especially for the early 70's. They were Italian, so beautiful. The Oak Bay Toy Shop was well the cat's meow for superior playthings.

One of them, Cecilia was a big crying baby doll in an exquisite carriage. Then there was Fiona, with a shag hair cut and Angela, a tall silver blonde. The one male doll I had was named Tony, who actually looked a lot like my future first husband of the same name. Just like in the Nutcracker Suite when the dolls grew up!

I loved birds very much, literally spending hours observing them with my grandfather's binoculars.

Each Saturday morning I would hammer with wood left over from the builders, birdhouses and feeders.

There were many various square and smooth shaped wood pieces that went naturally in place. The knots from the previouse branches of the trees made a perfect birdhole. I had a windmill feeder and a bird cafeteria made from long boards. On the front I wrote with crayons, BIRDLAND.

Though I was alone for hours at a time it didn't seem to matter. For it was a very special and happy little world I had created around myself.

Like a safe cocoon incubating creativity for an emerging butterfly. I always had something to do and I rarely felt lonely.

The big birch tree in the backyard was the monument where all this transpired. In the front there was the weeping willow where I had my own kind of natural condo. It had branches that cascaded right down like an umbrella opening into a woody world. The biggest thrill of my young life was when I would sometimes sneek out of bed to sleep under this willow tree. It was my own kind of natural condo.

My time was beautifully consumed with school, fantasy, birds, music and dance.

Whenever Minxie, my black cat or our other persian cat Princess sent a bird to Glory, I would have a nice Anglican like funeral; all under that willow tree. Inevitably, Birdie Burial was reverently done with a wing and a prayer.

Whenever I think about how rich and simple my

Dreams night

childhood was, I rediscover that simplistic richness a...
apply that principle in my life now!

Through all this outward life of normality I was
involuntarily engaged in the unseen realm. I was only six
years old when the visitations or satanic nightmares were
tormenting me. These were no ordinary childhood
nightmares. The blazing red, hideous type. I remember one
in particular in which I was so sure that my room was ablaze
with fire. Another in which lucifer appeared to me horns and
all. He said to me "Go to hell!" "Go to hell!"

I was moving backwards in space and dimensions. Like
dreams you as readers have probably had. I tried to call
out... but I couldn't utter a sound. In another so called
nightmare, satan took me down to the door of hell, which I
remember had a big knocker on it. The natural gargoyle
type! Each night I didn't want to go to sleep because I knew
I'd immediately go into a frightening realm.

I'll tell you directly, I may not be frightened now of lucifer
as a powerful christian in the conscious realm; but then and
now in the unconscious realm, he's very horrible and
dangerous, no matter how tough you are. Here, I am a small
child. There was no education in our home, of how to defend
yourself in prayer, Jesus nothing.

I know that most of the time I didn't tell a soul what I was
seeing and what was visiting me in my bedroom.

Most nights before I went to sleep, there would be this
"presence" over my bed. Almost like near breathing. I also
had distinct physical pinches in my side every night. Keep in
mind that when I had these pinches, I wasn't totally asleep
yet! The bizarre thing is whenever I awoke out of a
nightmare, when I drifted back into sleep I was right back to
where it left off.

When I was eight, I was taken to Sunday school and I enjoyed it! I loved chapel in private school. In fact when the kids were fooling around in class I thought to myself; You shouldn't be like that, these people are special; (Jesus, Mary, John etc) they deserve our respect! I was destined then for the Lord's Kingdom. I can see The Thread of things here and there pertaining to my salvation. For years I loved to sing and swing which I'd do for hours. Grandma had Mr. Shattinger (The German construction worker who built our house.) make a simple but absolutely beautiful swing with a big wooden frame. I would sing and swing so high! Siegfried our less than normal Doberman Pincher, would like to try and grab my heels pulling me off the swing! I was of course terrified! He was a really nervous weird dog. We totally believed later that Sigfried in his instability became demonically possessed. As all these things were transpiring, starlings were nesting in what mom called "The starling shanty." I painted this birdhouse in blue and red with water colors from school. There was a small field from our house, that I loved where I'd catch grasshoppers and bottle them. It had a small tree that I swung up and down on. I thought that it was really special to climb up its' branches and gaze over the city in the warm summer sunshine. When the long grass was mowed I and my best friend, Christina would make a hay fort. I could be quite secluded in there.

Our next door neighbours were the Russels and to the right of us the Grahams. Mr. Stan Graham seeme to be a person after my own heart. He made birdhouses too and in fact he built me one for the sparrows. A sparrow "couple" were house shopping and looked at it. The husband tried to squeeze his little self in, but was too fat. So was his wife. Too much birdseed on a bun I guess! I don't know if any sparrows could muster to fit into the small hole that Mr. Graham had drilled in. The Grahams had about four different types of berries. There was loganberries, strawberries, and of course we both had blackberries at the back of our fences. He'd invite my mother and my brother Mark to pick some pails full. We froze them and had them as jam or put straight onto ice cream. As well they had peaches growing on a climber on the side of their house and orange pippin' apples. They are a special type of apple with a unique taste. Added to this fruitopia were vegetables, red skinner green beans. Sometimes they were as long as a twelve inch ruler. Rhubarb was also an indulgence. It was this vegetable, where I first learned that the leaves were deadly poisonous. The Graham's had their yards impeccably kept. The lawn in the back was manicured like an emerald green carpet. The front had a lovely variety of heavenly blossoming roses.

The greatest project Mr. Graham accomplished was the six foot tall handmade windmill. I still remember him steadily working on it in his basement for months. When it was finished it was so beautiful. They dressed me in a Dutch outfit they'd had from their travels and I stood beside it. Looking like I could pass for a little Dutch girl with my platinum blonde hair and fair skin.

I'd play their organ occasionally, and one time they recorded it with my singing and sent it down to their relatives in California. They thought I had been professionally trained for years. I was making it up and was only twelve at the time. Their home was a cozy kind of place, with trinkets neatly displayed. These were from their holiday travels. Downstairs there were shells and starfish. Their house's exterior was covered with coloured broken glass. I used to think that alot of broken bottles were needed to do that! The Graham's were quiet, kind older people who were especially meaningful to me. They added a new and needed dimension to my little life. I was alone a lot of the time since there were no kids in our neighbourhood my age. I was creating a world of my own. I'm still doing it to this very day, except of course the stakes are higher, I do it in the areas of business, and entreprenurial pursuits. In moments of melancholy, or isolation, I still turn to my music and dancing if I have the room! Its been a good life, but also an extremely difficult one. That's O.K. I'm more accepting now. Anyway I hope I am.. because I know one thing for sure, that God is wonderful!! In between good times I seemed to be a "magnet" for rejection by other children and people. Though on the other hand I have also been adored, and been popular, mostly in my later years. But the entrenched rejection, would later on feed into an already disturbed condition and unstable complex of myself. As a child I was ill quite often. One Christmas I remember standing on the scales to see my 5' 1" frame register at 75 lbs. I had pnemonia. I was away from school for two weeks, going back briefly to our class's Christmas party. I slowly ate a few things on my paper plate, then after in a stupor I waited for my mother on the steps of the school.

Allergies were my pretty constant, unpredictable adversary. Dust, cat hair, pollen bee stings, etc. would make my eyes swell shut and my mouth became huge with the swelling of edema. Sometimes I'd be almost blind for a couple of days. I couldn't go on camping trips till I was fifteen. I was taken for those "world famous" allergy tests the ones in which they make a myriad of scratches on your back and you end up looking tattooed at an early age! They're vials of various substances to see what you react to. Penicillin was the most dangerous allergy for me. A more recent but none the less horrific allergic attack occured from mowing the lawn. I apparently had a reaction to the moist mold in the under layer of the grass and an edema filled, egg shaped lump appeared on the back of my neck. My hands swelled like rubber gloves with water in them. Our G.P. said they don't know why later on in life we have different allergies than as a child and why we grow out of some. Then we acquire completely different ones in another part of our body.

As a child I was a very free spirit, a total individual. I still am. Society doesn't really support individuality or sensitivity. Believe me individuality and sensitivity may be great for the arts but it's a killer in the world! If you are either one or both, you know what I'm talking about. My brother Mark was quite the opposite. He had to have people always around him and had to be couched by my grandmother with his school projects etc. He was an incredible baseball player and we have pictures of him when he was barely 10 with trophies, in Little League. Mark was an awesome pitcher. He once told my mom that he had actually thought of going professional with a career. Sadly because of the drug culture prevalent then, this was never to be, with many other things that were trashed because of the path he took.

My grandmother and my mother both played the piano beautifully. My grandma would play, "Puff The Magic Dragon" and we would sing it in harmony together. My mother achieved her Grade 10 in piano. She has three university degrees from the University Of Manitoba. One of them is a Bachelor Of Psychology. My mother has been a teacher, then a special counselor in all of the school districts in Victoria. This has been over a twenty year career. Now of course at the writing of this book, she has been retired for quite awhile. She took early retirement from the stressful family situation that had continued. It continued to be unusually hard for my small family, such is the "pilgrimage" of our lives.

My grandmother had a tendency to be a bit too tough in the disciplinary realm as with my piano practicing. I had to practice "The Etude" piano piece twice a day with a gun to my head so to speak. So when I had finally had it, the Etude and a Doberman Pinscher book had a nice bonfire! I wasn't a brat or anything, but I did have a smile on my face when I felt my torture was over!

CHAPTER 4

In 1979 Dr. Abram Hoffer, internationally known speaker on biochemistry and orthomolecular psychiatry gave up all hope on me after he had done all the treatments. Meds, hospitalization, shock treatments, etc. He said and I quote; "I am at the end of my rope with Louanne, Mrs. Metcalfe." "You have to take her to a church with a healing ministry." I was only fourteen, when my illness was at its' peak. Yet I was developing the "signs" as early as eleven years old. My mother first had schizophrenia when I was only eleven years old. You can imagine how disturbed this would cause a young child.

Dr. Hoffer said that she was one of the most ill patients he had seen! My mother here a brilliant, refined intellectual. She has been an interior designer, with the previously mentioned other credits. I am very proud of my mother. She is true to the word; "Lady."

Well with this dreadful disease she was incapacitated to

the point of not being able to even write her own name, drive the car etc.

It all seemed to start one night when we were in the kitchen of our house on 1512 Mc Rae Ave in Victoria, B.C. My mother had taken out some cranberries from the freezer which had been there for quite some time. She was planning to cook them and then I saw the distinct change in her. She said in a trembling half hysterical voice; "They might poison Lou Anne!" "They may be deadly and poison Lou anne!"

No, I knew this wasn't my mother anymore. Very hard on an 11 year old especially a mental illness, which is biochemical and very spiritual.

I am going to go through the symptoms we both had, the differences between hers and mine. Above all hopefully break the ignorance regarding it. What it is and what it is not. Most especially to "SHINE" Jesus light on it.

My mother became a nervous chain smoker, her beautiful long-tapered fingers were deeply stained yellow. To this day, I have never seen such intense staining. She was terrified of water on her body, wouldn't eat, hardly slept, heard voices, suffered from depression and the list goes on. Some of the symptoms we had were different. There is so much the doctors still don't know about schizophrenia. What it is and what it is not. There are "revelatory facts" about or should I say in the "real world of mental illness." These things are not known, but sadly to say are knowingly shunned by the medical establishment.

CHAPTER 5

Because as a BLUNT FACT each psychward with each bed, each shock treatment, each prescription of the myriad tranquilizers, anti-depressants, equals a nice whack of money!! Sadly, and even worse is the UNHOLY ALLIANCE of the psychiatrist with the pharmaceutical companies. Actually renaming well known neuroleptics, with NEW NAMES, changing some of these pills from blue to pink in colour and now rushing them through the mandatory screening processes. Thus putting the public at risk. This is all for the GOLDEN CALF, in actual LEGAL DISREGARD for the safety, and ultimate wellbeing of these unsuspecting victims. I could go on with the research I have done in this matter, how psychiatry is a 4.5 Trillion dollar a year industry! This no exaggeration, these are statistical facts. How I have seen with my own eyes, deaths, murders, suicides, brain atrophy, lives put on hold indefinitely. All this by the unmonitored, factory like pushed pills into the market. It's been called an Industry Of Death. Heavy statement, where each doctor, dating back to the the 1800's was required to take an OATH FOR THE WELL BEING OF PATIENTS TO THE BETTERMENT OF HUMAN LIFE THROUGH THE AGENT OF MEDICINE. Mental illness is a fast track to living on the street! It is said that between 35 & 75% of those that are homeless in Edmonton, ALONE (HOW MUCH THE REST OF THIS PLANET!) approximately 3,000 persons, have a serious mental illness including many with schizoprenia. We walk by them everyday.That wrecked looking man or woman pushing a shopping cart may not be homeless due to a lack of housing. Yet lack of affordable housing definitely compounds the problem. Yet it is not the main problem. So here we have some people not getting ANY TREATMENT AT ALL, WHILE OTHERS ARE GETTING WAY TOO MUCH DAMAGING SO CALLED TREATMENT. To again put it BLUNTLY. They are just pawns in the mighty chess board, orchestrated by money hungry, so called professionals. Who could really care less about their patients. It's these drugs that are raking in the doe. Tell me if they really cared, like the rare Dr. Hoffer did, why do they keep a poor patient of theirs waiting sometimes 25 mins extra for a scheduled appointment only to listen to them for maybe 10 mins, (There was a time when psychiatrists actually listened to their patients with some adequate counselling skills and compassion) then take out their fat prescription pad, and write another drug to add to the already large cocktail of neuroleptics their poor sap of a patient is already on. Then Bye Bye, and out the door for another, guy in their leather seat to have the same pathetic pattern that day repeated. Then Dr. so and so, gets a message from his receptionist that his wife called and he is late in booking their Honolulu

(meds)

vacation, for next week. HELLO? Something seriously wrong with this picture? Who cares, eh? Well the ones who fall mentally ill, saying, Oh it will never happen in my family, we have it all together, we have social skills, strong ethnic background, on and on. Then it happens and you are in the other chair. THE PATIENT ELECTRIC CHAIR! Can't happen? That's what we thought… You never know in life, so be prepared, this book should do more for those ill right at this moment, to those that WILL BECOME ILL. IT'S A FACT IN OUR WORLD, ESPECIALLY NOW. There's way more "media" factors, like computer video games, virtual reality movies, that are down right DANGEROUS SPIRITUALLY AND EMOTIONALLY, that we never had when I grew up, yet LOOK HOW SICK I WAS. There is more out there to TIP VULNERABLE SOULS AND YOUNG MINDS THAN EVER IN THE HISTORY OF THE WORLD!! So if we see a lot more young people firing shots at their classmates, taking a whole school hostage, children murdering grownups, more grisly murders than can be imagined, insanity on our street, (That man harassing you for a few coins when you're entering London Drugs, when all you want is to get that designer make-up, your kids, some chocolate to shut them up.)well I wonder WHY? Unfortunately what I observe now is a TIDAL WAVE OF CRITICAL PROPORTIONS THAT ONE WOMAN'S VOICE (Mine) can do a lot, but I need you ALSO BEHIND ME TO START A REVOLUTION, THAT IS INEVITABLE, TO TURN THE DESTRUCTIVE PATH OF DEATH, AND TRAGEDY, THAT HAS TO BE INTERCEPTED, WITH THIS DRUGGING TO OBLIVION, APPROACH. Note, I don't even mention the word treatment here, it's not treatment it's TORTURE. I will not elaborate anymore at this time on this, only to say, I have NO RESPECT FOR THOSE, WHO USE OTHERS TO WHATEVER DISASTER IN THE END, FOR THEIR OWN WICKED GREEDY GAIN. And neither should any decent, human being with a whisp of conscience. By the way, Hitler not only massacred the jews, ukranians, armenians etc, he ordered his appointed doctors in the experiments and torture of the mentally ill. He said that the schizophrenics, the old, the retarded are useless eaters and it would be best to exterminate all of them. Wow nice guy. Yet gee whiz we never hear about that do we? It's a hidden, researched FACT.

Anyway as my mother digressed into a worsening state, she was more like a zombie and her clothes were becoming looser each passing day. She noticed this while she was bravely still going to her work. She said that she had a subtle sweat emanating from her upper body downwards. My mother had over twenty shock treatments;(Over a period of course of time.) (ECT's) After this she immediately believed in the reality of Almighty God!! She felt wonderful! Now though note she had been sick for over a year and had extensive megavitamin therapy, with mild corresponding neuroleptics. Recovery from schizophrenia perhaps more than the other mental illnesses, (like manic depression,) is slow and very painful. One of the many factors are the withdrawal from the drugs and the "shock" of the veil being lifted off the illness itself.

CHAPTER 6

We have been immeasurably blessed to have had the best orthomolecular psychiatrist in the world. I have the biggest file in Dr. Hoffer's office to this day, though he has hundreds of patients. Doesn't that say alot? I had quite different symptoms from my mother's. She wasn't suicidal, (Though of course she wanted to die.) I was extremely volatile in this regard. I almost accomplished my goal numerous times. I self inflicted myself with butcher knives to my legs and arms, broken light bulbs to my wrists, and overdoses. Throwing myself down balconies etc. In the early stages, Dr. Hoffer thought I had subpelliminal pellagra, a deficiency disease.

Yet soon he could see that it was much more than that.

Schizophrenia is a three-fold disease, very much body, mind and soul. At least with the other diseases of the "physical" you have your mental capacity or faith. Though I don't in any way downplay the suffering and seriousness of these illnesses. This one though is so all encompassing, that nothing is free from the merciless torture. My mother used to say it was like being shredded inside. So true. The worse it is the more you suffer and the more delicate, sensitive you are the more agony as well.

The term SCHIZOPHRENIA, as Dr. Hoffer says in his book; "How To Live With Schizophrenia" is not a good terminology at all. The term implies that something is DIVIDED or SPLIT. But the personality is not divided or split any amount of times. \par

The originator of the term was Eugene Bleuber referring to a lack of connection between the thinking and the feeling of the patient. Also the meaning of it as used by journalists and writers is an error. The adjective schizophrenia is becoming a part of our language to mean separateness as in; "schizophrenic nation" schizophrenic attitudes, schizophrenic politics. Used in this way it may impart some vague meaning to the reader yet actually has no meaning in relation to the disease from which it is derived. There's an older term; Dementia Praecox or precocious or parboiled madness. Of course the term is Latin. This concept from sixty years ago, now serves no useful purpose. On the contrary alot of trouble and stigma has been instigated by this terminology. It's not accurate to a symptom or a disease and will some day be replaced by more suitable diagnostic terms. Just as "fevers" were replaced as a diagnosis by definite diseases. Public education can teach people that there is nothing to fear in (names) themselves. Tuberculosis was once feared for the same illogical reasons we now fear schizophrenia. There are of course serious differences. I believe strongly that society as a whole has an innate fear, abhorrence if you will, to the lack of functioning of the mind (Horror of insanity) more than the physical diseases where the mind is still intact so to speak.

CHAPTER 7

FACT:

What schizophrenia is and what it is NOT.

To Begin With; #1 Schizophrenia is not the parents fault. This Freudian scapegoat principle as used by psychiatrists harms not only the individual (the patient) but all concerned. Especially family.

#2 It is not caused by something being astray in the personality. Many diseases went through this stage at one time, including general attitudes toward the insane. Fortunately medicine (Thanks to our doctors) brought them into proper focus, before they ran rampant over our society.

#3 All classes of society can have schizophrenia. It is not just prevalent to the poor as once thought. It is in all cultures and societal structures. Fairly distributed among all races of men. No matter where they are. In fact you will find the largest percentage of those with this illness are "Elite people." Intellectuals highly creative, often geniuses. Brilliant and in a sense-fragile minds. I like to call them crystal cerebullums or glass menageries. Like the title of the excellent movie based on a true story of John Nash, "A Beautiful Mind". He was the man that changed the face of our economics and mathematics. \par

When I say fragile I believe because they are bright and finely attuned in AWARENESS. Very exceptional alot of the time with undetected by the rest of humanity, skills in symbolism, subtle details and subliminal undercurrents. In a variety of subjects. Lets face it they also have the patience. Life is not superficial or casual to these people! Not just your highly intelligent businessman or ruler. You will find them as painters, writers, musicians, singers, poets or a combination of all of these. They can usually do . several things simultaneously and all to a high quality of professionalism. I believe it is high time that these valuable people were treated far kinder the way Jesus would treat them and nurture their gifts. This with the knowledge of nutrition, vitamin supplementation, and spirituality would go farther than psychiatry alone has. Ever has gone.

I personally do not agree with the notion in books on this subject that it is not triggered or complicated by "stress." For my mother and I are a living example that it isn't helped one bit by stress. Especially non-relenting stress. I became ill from the relentless stress of school persecution, pressure and family difficulties. The bomb that affected my mother's health was her job and particularily the escalating pressure of my brother's criminal behaviour, drug and alcohol use. Often she was having to go to juvie court. These factors are crystal clear in my mind and there is a definite pattern of cause and effect. Still to this day I cannot handle intense stress for prolonged periods. Now there is a difference in what kind of stress we HEALED schizophrenics can and cannot handle. Stress connected with my craft, that of musical practice and performance, or putting myself under my own pressure of a schedule for writing or physical exercise. Jobs in society do not seem to have a very long duration for me. Not anything else that I am not physically or psychologically able to withstand. If you think about it stress is a "breaking down" thing, it depends on how much stamina you have to bear under it. It is one of the greatest killers in the world today. So if your regular Joe with stronger resistance can't handle it, how much more those of a delicate constitution? I've had to learn many things as a healed, delivered former mental patient and Born Again Christian. One thing that I have taken in the scripture too intensely is "I can do all things through Christ who strengthens me." Yes, I've taken that a little too far sometimes! Hey that's better than saying I don't have zeal or am lukewarm! Definitely not.

CHAPTER 8

I forced myself to do some things and they weakened me so much physically that I temporarily collapsed and then what re-entered? That old enemy depression and then with that lies in my mind from the devil. Yes, this disease is biochemical but genetically inherited? The Lord revealed firsthand to a lady that it was demonically inherited. Something that would really flip the wigs of psychologists and psychiatrists! You will find this information in the back of the book; "Pigs In The Parlour" I don't know if it's still on the market. I'll tell you briefly what it says: A visual example of a ten-fingered hand representing the amount of demonic spirits connected with it. The first is the "Spirit of rejection"

Some people reading this may find this is going too far or even that it's "demon chasing" or they've heard through ignorant channels. It doesn't matter. I believe anything the Lord specifically reveals to a sound, honest reliable Christian. Besides when you have experienced something first hand and have almost died from it, you are the best

AUTHORITY on it. That's what I firmly believe. Plus each person that I've talked to that have had serious depression almost always had it back in their family. Uncle so and so killed himself or grandpa was depressed alot etc. Melancholy they used to say alot in the so called "Good ole days?" Why the answer is of "Curses" being placed on families. Yes curses. The roots can go way back to where you originated from. Then the spiritual condition and atmosphere of that country or place. Ireland. This country for example, has apparently been full of schizophrenia. Here \ul \ulnone we have a \ul \ulnone paradox, they can be into witchcraft and the occult. Yet in this country we have the strongest strain of the Catholic church in the world!! And documented appartions of Jesus, Mary, St Michael with messages to warn mankind!! I'm not going to go into denominations here and what any of us "think" of that church whatever, just the blatant facts. The fight of good and evil! Darkness and Light. I believe the demons under satan's command are sent to seek out vulnerable, highly attuned minds. Well nobody could have been more vulnerable as a child that I was.

I mean we're out there, it's just not your MAJORITY. Musicians particularily as portrayed in the Bible had numerous accounts of importance in the front of the literal ARMIES led by Joshua, for an example especially throughout the Old Testament. This is rich IN THE REALM OF SPIRITUAL FORCES DEALT WITH IN THE UNSEEN REALM. Then manifested in the natural.

Fortified walls around an enemy city was brought down not with a literal bulldozer but a SPIRITUAL STRATEGIC ONE. The walls of Jericho came down in seven days by a marching of the troops and blowing of trumpets. The prestige and Holy respect given to musicians of critical importance in Biblical times is something society and even the church has lost to this day. I want this to be restored to its rightful place. The account of Nebuchadnezzar's depression and torment was only alleviated by King David's singing and playing of the harp. They have always said that music can tame the savage beast!! So it is.

I believe the devil knows who could have the potential for being a mighty warrior for the Lord. So why not kill them off as quickly as possible?

CHAPTER 9

Two thought processes that occur in schizophrenia are;

#1 The thought process may be slowed down. Frequently in patients who are severely depressed.

#2 A marked acceleration of thought which more typical of 'manic' states. This is what the experts say may account for the increased BRILLIANCE of many young patients when the illness is just beginning. I remember when I was only three years old I was sitting for a professional photographer and he had to get me to hold a glass toy ball with some object in it. This was so he could get my attention straight on. My mind and eyes were all over the place. He said, "Her mind is like mercury." My daughter Rebecca, was the same way. She exhibited remarkable awareness at infancy. I have had trouble with people trying to understand me because my mind works faster than my mouth. Though my mouth works pretty fast! So I usually have to repeat to people all over again. My mother and I share the same "Hi Speed internet connection!"

#3. A common symptom of schizophrenia is thought processes that are so disturbed that there is one thought followed by another with no direct connections. Thoughts may jump at random. Memory and recall may become so disturbed that clear thinking becomes impossible. It's interesting to think of the scriptures in regards to this line, \'c4 Double Minded Man Is Unstable In All His Ways. (Or woman of course) How the mind is often discussed in Christian literature as the battle ground of our spiritual warfare. "Biochemically speaking" how NIACIN is the fundamental vitamin for schizophrenia. Niacin goes directly to the brain and of course the nervous system. Dr. Hoffer said and I agree with him, that most of society's population should be on some amount of Niacin.

Why you may ask? Since the wheat to the bread that hold most of the B-vitamin, niacin has been through processing, bleaching and lousy soil. So you can see it is virtually depleted, if existing at all.

Chemicals, pesticides etc, has almost obliterated this vital, I repeat VITAL VITAMIN FROM THE EARTH! Every time in certain countries where the niacin was put back (Thus enriched on the package label) into the bread, people in that region who had started to exhibit signs of schizophrenia, well they quickly recovered. This is facts that I have researched meticulously. Then again where this key nutrient was non-existent in the farmland there was a disturbing percentage of people not well. Of course those who have what's called a predispositional potential in their biochemical and heredity make up (Genes) to mental illness, they succumb first.

Niacin is called a "VASODILATOR" meaning it completely opens up all the ventricles in the brain and the nervous system, heart etc, causing unrestricted blood flow. Pushing out all obstructions. If you know about heart disease, or seizures, it's CRITICAL TO HAVE A STEADY FLOW OF BLOOD TO THESE AREAS, it's blood clots, irregular heart beats that cause heart attacks. Dr. Hoffer did more research on niacin and found that it even has proven to keep cancer cells from even forming!

So thus the reason of niacin causing its famous burning flush!! This is very important to endure and get past. This is proof of it's effectiveness. After a few years on a regimented daily dose after every meal of the appropriate milligrams (Different for every individual.) this flushing almost disappears. It even becomes quite pleasant like a "Rush" affect that is looked forward to. Hey if people like getting "High" on Drugs on the street that kill brain cells, why not get high on a vitamin that even grows new ones and makes you more intelligent and faster in all areas? Makes sense. I still am astounded and even infuriated by those who try to keep this info from the public that it is dangerous harms the liver etc, Look I've taken it for over 30 years, and I am still alive!! In fact people take me always for up to 15 year younger than my age, since I was on it so early and it is known to dramatically slow down the aging process. I'm in incredible physical shape, have thick still, golden blonde hair, no lines on my face and do sports that many women half my age, can't do as fast as I do. I'm half way to 50 and I look maybe 30! Convinced you? Now you'll want to shut your ears to your spouse, doctor and all who say no to niacin and run down to your local drugstore and get a couple bottles of this (cheap too!) MIRACLE VITAMIN, AND

THROW A MEAL DOWN YOUR THROAT AND START ON AT LEAST TWO PILLS AND HAVE THE RUSH AND YOUTH FOUNTAIN FLOW!! It's funny and I am a great believer in humour except this one is true!! Know someone exhibiting signs of mental illness, they are in a danger zone, TELL THEM ABOUT NIACIN, PROPER DIET AND THE OTHER VITAMINS I HAVE DISCUSSED, THE B VITAMINS, ETC, VIT C. Time is of the essence with mental illness. It insidiously creeps up and is dangerous and to be taken very seriously. I should know it almost took my life!! and my mother's.

After the flushing is almost nonexistent except the times you are inactive (it seems to hit harder when you haven't moved around much in the day) obviously having to do with the circulation factor, which I find fascinating. So when this is not exhibiting, THE FLUSH, THE ROYAL FLUSH! then this is a good sign of your body and brains adjustment successfully to your particular amounts. (I'm meaning milligrams) It has passed the threshold I call it and the assimilation has been successful. Clearer thinking, more connection in thought processes, more ENERGY, burning off of carbs, alertness, happier mood are just some of the immediate blessings to look forward to. This thing of damage of too much niacin to your liver, is B.S. pure and simple. I would of died of liver disease along time ago. My organs are all in excellent condition. Any other problems I did have was from flu viruses, and infections in my stomach and bladder that went too long unaddressed.

The Royal Flush of the niacin is especially appreciated by my husband who is on it now. He works outside, and we live in Edmonton, AB. so with the winters, well you get my snow drift!! and for me it has prevented any arthritis, from this cold province from setting in. His premature arthritis in his legs, is cured since he started on niacin over 2 years ago!! He looked like a bow legged cowboy, and now he can pretty well keep up with me on my power walks. This is also on top of sometimes his 10 hour days. He does not do a sit down job, and he is well into his 50's again people think he is in his forties. Even his hair that was going grey, when he started the niacin, almost overnight, tresses of his natural strawberry blond hair, came in bushels, and his moustache was like Redbeard, flaming red!! The lines normally around any man over 50 and in a dry climate, vanished. Well that sold Richard, I didn't have to do any blackmail or beating over the head, like I've had to do with my other friends to convince them of the fabulous effects of niacin. He said he found the youth fountain, and put himself on a higher dose than me!! He has more energy, than the guys at his work that are more than half his age. He got this job, coming from B. C. in three days, and in ONE YEAR HE WAS EMPLOYEE OF THE MONTH TWICE!! He has a hard working ethic, (British background) but also the vitamins, combined with a rich fish oil every day has made an obvious dramatic difference. Believe me people have noticed.

I personally rarely have a flushing experience unless I've been inactive, that particular day. I've been on 4,500 mg for over 30 years. Hello!

CHAPTER 10

Now in regards to schizophrenia again it is very important, in fact CRITICAL that the early warning signs of

1. Deep depression, anxiety and any bizarre behaviour is heeded seriously, WITH COMPASSSION AND GREAT CARE. If someone in your family or anyone else you know may seem to be manifesting this get them to a doctor, RIGHT AWAY. Preferably, a doctor who believes in vitamins and nutrition, at least one who has an open mind. An orthomolecular psychiatrist if possible is the most desired obviously. Combined with this the Christian church. One with some discernment and insight into theses matters. Not one that will say you can go off all your pills and just have Jesus. It has to be balanced, sane. I still am vigilant with both. If I \ i slip up on either one I pay for it. \ i0 You cannot go lone ranger with one approach in this type of disease.

Reading in "Pigs In the Parlour" book it is very important to bring the identity of Jesus and who the person is as as an

individual soul. Created in the IMAGE OF GOI
reality to those who take the scriptures of Genesi
in a careful process of time. I believe schizophrer
potentially to become ill, are very spiritual peopie. reople
that could go either way. I know I had what's called
"clairvoyant ability" Since I can remember. Seems to run in
families.

My grandmother had the Gift."
I was recently told by a friend (Quite my senior)if I hadn't
become a Christian I could of been like a witch. Or with just
straight E.S.P. powers. No title attached. I do have a strong
GIFT when it comes to dreaming precognitively. I keep
journals of my dreams and over 90% have come to pass. This
is a high accuracy rate. I used to be pretty good at mind
reading. We used to do it once in a while around the kitchen
table after dinner. As well tea cup reading and horoscopes
were part of our little family. Of course not at all very good
for our household spiritually.

Sun. Sept. 30th 2012
Leaving N.C.

CHAPTER 11

Getting back to the chemistry of the brain; There is another mood besides depression and that is MOOD FLATNESS. It is produced in the body and is the caused by the hormone ADRENALINE. The only hallucinogens (Drugs capable of producing hallucinations as in schizophrenia) They are adrenochrome and adrenolution. These are two compounds formed from the hormone adrenaline, which are probably present in the body and which the doctors think are somehow responsible for the disease process of this illness.

I want to counteract the "myth" that schizophrenics are dangerous. They are more of a danger to themselves than other people. The risk of homicide among them is no greater than for non-schizophrenics. It is a general rule that a violent aggressive patient is a sign of poor psychiatric treatment. Yet we can never generalize and I acknowledge situations of particular reasons that violence to others has indeed occurred. as in Dr. Hoffer's book "How To Live With

Schizophrenia" regarding the chemicals in the body. "The body factory" which used up chemicals and produces other chemicals which must be different from that of a normal subject. In that it must have the capacity to GO OUT OF ORDER for some reason. Thus starting biochemical changes in motion. That is why I have previously stated that it is so terribly important that the medical side of it not be brushed aside. Churches well meaning, but ignorant, say that the Lord is the Great Physician and all you need is His healing touch. So you can throw out all your pills, eat whatever you like and all is well! No I don't thing so! These souls that get ill with this dreadful scourge, have a very different nervous system and biochemistry than the rest of society. God intended for us to listen to our doctors. Why would He create them? You can't always separate the body and mind from the spirit. Just as an example; my system is apparently rather rare. The side effect of some drugs in a certain way have the opposite affect on me to what is "labelled" for the majority. You see what I'm trying to convey? Before I became ill, I was very allergic. I was unusually susceptible to the environment in a variety of ways and my blood came out "High" in this allergic sensitivity. Particularily in the area to bacteria. I had confirmed by my G.P. that my immune system is not the strongest, and needs a vigilant boost continually. Interesting that when I was ill, the allergies disappeared almost completely . This is one of the biochemical changes that occur in this particular illness. No more childhood allergies. As I started to become well they returned. Interesting isn't it? Your hormones are off balance with this disease. The main ones involved with this disease are ADRENALIN which turns into ADRENOCHROME. Then from that it's changed into two new compounds; leuco-adrenochrome, which is harmless and the other adrenolutin which is poisononous. Dr. Hoffer said my body was full of poison, very toxic.

CHAPTER 12

There was one Christmas I want to forget forever. Yet I must share it with you to help you and others. It was a Black Christmas. I could not move or even lift my head off the pillow. My dear mother brought all my presents to the hospital, which was so packed with patients at that time that my bed was in the hall with a curtain around it. Well I couldn't do the simplest thing, like opening them. My mother had to do it for me. This gave her a brutal revelation of my critical condition. Now Dr. Hoffer is (was recently passed away) an orthodox Jew, yet he referred my mother to take me to a church quote; "With a healing ministry." "Mrs. Metcalfe I'm at the end of my rope with Lou Anne." He thought of the church because of a former patient similiar to me. A blonde woman, married, a pianist that had recovered through the church. Her husband had devotedly taken her. It was the whole nine yards with this torturous disease of the devil. I became violent and was put into a completely enclosed room with no windows. A mat to sleep on the hard floor. My diner was on a styrofoam tray shoved under the door. To defficate it wa a bedpan. I was only fourteen years of age, the youngest patient on the ward. They hadn't designed the area for the adolescents yet. They had a children's floor but of course I had crossed the "Threshold" of the required age.

Paranoia is a well known symptom in mental illnesses. Everywhere I went I felt strongly that people were staring at me. Sometimes they were truly laughing at me. So later on when people were enjoying their own personal joke together, I was so tense thinking it was me that was the object of their humour. To be honest it took years even when I was healed to get over that. It's like being gun—shy from being in Aushwitz or some War. I mean the battle continues even after healing and that is reintegrating oneself to society again. You see you've been in another world quite awhile and in the PROTECTIVE ATMOSPHERE of the hospital. Now all barriers are down. It's very hard and scary at times. You feel like a fresh piece of fragile pottery or glass china. Then you're sent out with the pots and pans. I was on an antidepressant till I was twenty. If I became depressed because of the inevitablilities of life, I would do some good vigorous exercise or singing my lungs out! Very fortunate to be a musician. Excellent indeed.

CHAPTER 13

Regarding the area of smoking it never really interested me. The biochemical facts regarding smoking is that every time a person smokes, substantial amounts of adrenaline are released in the body. You know what I previously said about adrenaline; it is not good for schizophrenics. Especially a rapid RUSH EFFECT. Also smoking draws vitamins; C & B from your system. You need to be able to store up the "B" vitamins. Vitamin C is never stored in the body so vigilant intake is appropriate. You can take 1000 mg every hour with NO HARM, I REPEAT NO HARM TO ANY ORGAN OR AREA OF YOUR BODY, FACT. In fact concentrated amounts of Vitamin C taken with diligence every day will strengthen the tendons in the bottom of the feet. Certain flus, infections and now the more resilient strains of viruses and SUPERBUGS, I find need a good "Whack" with say garlic or liquid oregano, (Strong herbal formula that annihilates, all bad bacteria, but has a huge list of other benefits, hypoglycemia, diabetes, arthritis among others.)

Garlic and liquid oregano are both POWERFUL NATURAL ANTIBIOTICS AND ANTIMICROBIALS. The great thing about the natural herbal remedies is no side effects. Like yeast infections for women, which then requuire acidophilus pills or tons of yogourt to balance out the bacterial tract.

Synthetic antiobiotics are powerful, but cause a breakdown in the immune system so susceptible to things like skin rashes or other ailments. I find when I've had to go on the erthromycin, or tetracyline antibiotics, I seem to have the SHIELD of my immune system lowered and I start getting sore throats, skin rashes etc, etc. Garlic and ginger are a ROOT by the way. Ginger is medicinal, when you think of gingerale you think of it used for nausea. It is a good detoxifier and deeply penetrates the chest area when you have bronchitis. Combinations become vast with herbal, and spice remedies. I am not going to go into the cookbook of medicinal cocktails, here. But what I've listed here should be of help.

Of course it goes without saying that you learn alot when you've had to be your own laboratory.

Next; it is dangerous particularily for the mentally ill to have a lack of sleep. This in itself can cause hallucinations and other symptoms commonly present in those ill. I personaly have always needed alot of sleep. I'm not going to analyze why, just as much as why some people can get by on 6 hrs or less a day and function.

As a little kid, at Christmas time, unheard of but true, my grandmother had to shake me awake. She joked that I was born asleep! So there is a great factor of probably an overdose of seratonin in my brain. The sleeping chemical, we all have amounts of it. It's located at the lower hippocampus beside the cerebullum.

Because my need for sleep is more than most people, (I still need 10-12 hrs sleep as an adult.) I tend to drive myself alot to get as much as I can accomplished the briefest periods of time. I now seem to have permanently unpredictable rollercoaster waves of energy and dissipation. Remember with due respect, that schizophrenic people are "fragile" emotionally. They should be treated accordingly to that factor with gentleness and empathy. Mercy should be there obviously. Otherwise their recovery may be slowed down or even reversed.

(The cayman wilderness)

CHAPTER 14

Who could be kinder than the Son Of God? But make no mistake, he was from God and God Himself is no push over, neither are we to be. It's a tricky tightrope, when to be righteously angry, confront people for injustice etc, and when to be quiet and turn the other cheek. It's for the appropriate circumstances, with the appropriate approach.

What I love especialy about Jesus is his emphasis on the downtrodden, the afflicted, the poor, elderly and the children. If you know the Bible, at all there was a man in there who would if living today, be labelled a schizophrenia. He had many demons in him. They said out of him when they encountered Jesus, "We are Legion, for we are MANY."

Hello? You may have read when the Lord cast them out into the swine that then ran over a cliff! This man was quite likely left all alone to fend for himself. Like too many mentally ill people are. Jesus was going to END HIS TORMENT!! This is what Jesus did with me. He saved me from the clutches of satan and definite annihilation. I mean

54

to be one of the most ill adolescents, then to be resurrected to life with so many talents. Well there has to be a very important purpose. One of these is this book. Not too many I know if ANY, have covered this ground and incorporated all these crucial facts, into one biochemical bible.

I was so fortunate to receive treatment as early as I did. For too any people receive treatment too late. I still see people that I was in the hospital with. It's what's called The Revolving Door Syndrome. In and out of the mental wards, drugs relapses etc. Walking like zombies. Here I am so miraculously "Delivered" and on top of it I am now more healthy than the average person. Above all I know who the Creator is.

Like most things in life it doesn't happen all at once. It takes time, painstakingly and full dedication and vigilance to your healing. I mean that in not taking your health for granted, and watching your own personal "triggers" for relapse, watching diet, continuing the program of vitamins etc. Sleep, staying away from stressful, or disturbing social activites, that are not conducive to mental or physical well being. After it's all over there is the indelible "MARK" of being through the crucible of mental illness, that remains with you for the rest of your life. I suppose that is why you must help others. FOR YOU HAVE THE TRUE ANSWERS.

I'm still that sensitive artistic child. Now I'm tempered with suffering. So I no am like a modern day Joshua, David or Joan Of Arc, (But I haven't thank God been burnt at the stake yet.) I AM A FEMALE WARRIOR!

Life is like a 'LABYRINTH' it can take you on a maze of deception and sidetracks. You find that so called imaginary fairytale adventure can ve a very real invasion of our so called

ONLY REALITY. I've sure found out that there are indeed PARALLEL DIMENSIONS INTERACTING WITH THIS PLANE. It just seems that only 'the sensitives' pick up on it. Then they find it far more of a wild ride!! than any science-fiction story could every convey. I should know; I stepped into it a long time ago.

CHAPTER 15

I see the inadequacies of the present "mental health system" that is unfortunately in some respects entrenched in the Dark Ages. I envision and personally want to SPEARHEAD a sanitarium kind of place that is more like a garden resort, than an institution. With fresh air, grounds to walk through and a garden. Taking away the place of complete enclosure. Replacing the rigidness of these poor souls not even having walking privileges, without the surveillance of a nurse! Also of course the psychiatrist's permisssion. THIS IS INHUMANE!

I see this place having specific occupational rooms where a specfic occupation is worked on. Such as a music room for the souls musically inclined. Another room with computers, fax machines, phones etc. All for these priceless people to partake of. Even to immerse themselves. The mentally ill have every right to respectful, and life enhancing therapy, answers, training as much as anyone else with disabilities, or other diseases. Particularily as I have said before, since they are usually geniuses. Do we not see what these people could contribute to the enrichment of the world? Quality, etc, and they are being RIPPED OFF OF THEIR LIVES AND POTENTIAL IN THIS SOCIETY. THIS HAS TO TAKE A 360' TURN ALREADY A TON OF YEARS HAVE BEEN LOST AND COUNTLESS PEOPLE TRASHED, WHICH WE WILL NEVER HEAR OF OR PARTAKE OF WHAT THEY WOULD HAVE HAD TO OFFER!

A VISUAL ARTISTRY ROOM, for painting, photography, sketching etc. Then A DANCE STUDIO with mirrors, a balancing bar the whole package.

The meals would consist of healthy food, partly from a vegetable garden that could very easily be in the back of the property of this superior facility. Funds could be consistently raised to keep the financial overhead at a minimum. This by some of the patients themselves. Those that are well enough to handle that. For example; selling their crafts, pottery, art or woodworks. Created at this facility. I was trying myself to get a concert off the ground, playing the piano and singing my compositions for a fund raiser in regard to the mental health system and facilities support. I was involved in several places this was of course in Victoria, B.C. Yet I seemed to be quite an original threat to the establishment. You know those who keep pumping the pills into the unsuspecting victims. Which keeps the psychiatrist's velvet wallets lined with the GREEN STUFF! The pharmaceutical companies are also not too happy of anything that might possibly make a dent into the improvement of the health of the mentally ill. Hey, doesn't everyone know it's BIG BUSINESS for people to remain ill? Like a Medical Mental Health Mafia. Each hospital bed rakes in thousands of dollars. Each prescription of a brain numbing neuroleptic keeps the psychiatrist of the

What About Bob's in the Bahamas. Yes, his mansion and the two or three mercedes well situated in the long driveway Each young psychiatrist I read about in the excellent book, "Toxic Psychiatry" that refused to do shock treatments on poor souls were asked to leave the active arena of the psychiatric realm. These young ones were so appalled by some of the results of this treatment, (The shocking and drugging for profit) Some said they didn't care that they were fired, they went into another field. For the price tag of the vegetables they beheld was too much for anyone with a human heart. THIS IS A TRAVESTY OF THE WORST KIND. Think about our Mozarts, Churchills and Einstein's, Vincent Van Gogh's Edgar Allan Poe's and the list goes on. Who as you probably clued into all had documented manic depression, or schizophrenia. Vincent Van Gogh particularily suffered, as well as Lord Byron, the poet. Vincent's father was a Christian minister, and Vincent desired to achieve a similiar calling along with his driven gift of painting. He chastised himself mercilessly that he was not achieving the required christian level, wrestling between psychotic delusions the Bible scriptures. I play Vincent, the famous musical piece. All the verses by Don Mclean do honor to Vincent. Very beautiful, poignant song I've ever heard done in respect to someone mentally ill and talented. Marilyn Monroes, if they all were zapped and drugged to oblivion, tell me how would we be blessed by their art, acting. Their critical achievements to the betterment of mankind? Your answer is as good as mine. In fact in my research, Marilyn or Norma Jean Baker (Her real name) had major childhood hallucinations. She was in a mental ward in between her movies and was steadily through the years to the time of her death, DRUGGED UP. As we all know her death is still unanswered, but I have my speculations as I'm sure you do. She had at least one psychiatrist and had been VICTIMIZED since the time of early childhood. With foster homes and off the wall so called christian foster care rapes etc. Marilyn's mother was mentally ill when Marilyn was just little. A fragile shell of a woman, I saw portrayed in the well overdue movie; "Norma Jean, The True Story" starring Ashley Judd.

As far as I know Marilyn's mother was left to die in an insane assylum.

Myself 1966 in my grandfather's shoes in Winnipeg

My brother Mark and I on our house steps, winter
in Winnipeg, Man. 1966 I was two years old

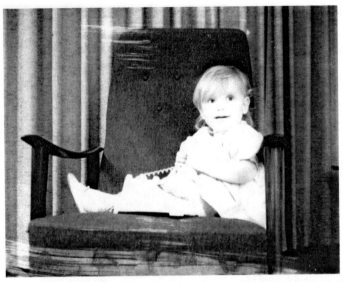

Myself at one years old sitting in my grandfather's chair 1965

My brother and I in Winnipeg, in the summer outside again 1966

Mark at 13 years old Superman, Junior High School picture 1974

Myself at Alberta Beach area 2009 Doing the Matrix thing!

My mother Margaret Anne at 50 years old

Mark and I doing cowboy and indians 1966 in our house in
Winnipeg, Man.

My guitarist and I having a dinner break after a performance, In
Victoria, B. C. 1992

CHAPTER 16

Now getting back to the nutritional aspect, megavitamins are actually a vitally required supplement that as I said previously said 80% of our society could definitely benefit from. Of course the levels of milligrams of each vitamin and mineral is specifically unique. As is each person's biochemistry. When those in power GENERALIZE AND STATE THAT WHAT IS RIGHT FOR A FEW INDIVIDUALS IS RIGHT FOR THE REST OF THE MASSES. THEN THEY ENFORCE IT, that is always a danger. You can refer to many things in history, not just with nutrition where this communistic way of thought has tried to put everyone into A MOLD. Humans, cannot be herded into a mass melting pot. It is precisely our uniqueness, and idiosyncracies that make the human race special. Unfortunately I have watched with an eagle eye, the pressure of conformity, (or be shafted) prevalent in an ever increasingly modern world. Technolgy has pros and cons, internet connecting to the vast world, yet on the other side of this coin it has also propogated some isolation, and far worse opportunites of crimial behaviour. Their is always a price tag to technological advancement. It seems to take away the human edge, and compassion.

With a world of fast food, processing, pesticides, quick growth gimmicks and pollution, is it any wonder that we have a allergic and deficient society. No a rocket scientist is not required here.

Actually the "term" MEGADOSE as Dr. Hoffer has spoken of has caused unnecessary havoc. It should be called OPTIDOSE. For Mega implies megaton, mega-truck. This seems to flip out people.

CHAPTER 17

Here is various material written by mentally ill persons. I can relate to a shocking degree to what they say and feel. It's very important to let you in on the different minds these people have. It's truly fascinating.

Here's Mary Maclene who is of course of Scottish descent. Quote; "I am a creature of intense, passionate feeling. I feel everything. It is my genius. It burns me like fire." Mary Maclen's genius of intense passionate feeling is in a sense the hot, white core of mental illness. Despite all of it's destructiveness and pain, the attempt to move into the realm of profound emotion is heroic. Which is perhaps synonymous with intense experiencing and existence as the one positive element in mental illness that we may understand and sympathize with. There is the suggestion that within mental illness human existence is being lived in its most intense, naked and real form. Real in the sense that it is unprotected by the structure of comforts and myths, which we call culture.

Also in the sense that whatever myths and delusions in terms of which one lives, are one's own productions. They are not borrowed that are disguised as social realities. Another quote by Mary; "Oh will the wise wide world give me in my outstretched hand a stone? " Hmm... yes I Louanne like Mary Maclean have quite an unusual intensity of life. The PAYBACK OF GOING THROUGH THE CRUCIBLE.

The sympathy that psychiatry has had for its patients has always been the sympathy of the well for the sick. It is a sympathy tinged with superiority, with a resitance to change. It seems to me that it is and overlording to change the person rather than the illness itself. Here is what Mary Maclean says of herself; "I of womanhood and of nineteen years, will now begin to set down as full and frank a portrayal I am able of myself." Mary Maclean for whom the world contains not a parallel." "I am convinced of this for I am odd." I am distinctly original, innately and in development.

"I have in me a quite unusual intensity of life." I can feel. I have a marvelous capacity for misery and for happiness. Can I ever relate to that.

"\ 'cf am broad minded."

"\ 'cf am a genius."

(Quotes of Mary Maclean)

I am a philosopher of my own good peripathetic school. My brain is a conglomeration of aggressive versatility. I know myself, oh very well. (So do I) Doesn't that help us survive?

"I have gone into the deep shadows.If all this constitutes oddity, I find therefore that I am quite, quite odd. I have hurt for even the suggestion of a parallel among the several hundred persons that I call acquaintances. But in vain. There are people of varying depths and intricacies of character but there is none to compare with me."Mary Maclean again. I wouldn't dare say that.. but she has every right, I don't mind it.

"The young ones of my own age, if I chance to give them but a glimpse of the real workings of my mind, can only stare at me in dazed stupidity." "Noncomprehending these are." As well the old ones of forty and fifty. You're always old at nineteen. They also stare at in stupidity. Or else their own narrowness asserting itself, smile their little devilish smile of superiority, which they reserve indiscriminately for all foolish young things. The utter idocy of forty and fifty at times! To be sure these are extreme instances. Others who understand some phases of my complicated character. Though none comprehend it in its entirety.

"Yet as I said, even the suggestion of a parallel is not to be found among them." Along certain lines I have gotten to the EDGE OF THE WORLD A step forward and I fall off. Not taking the step, I stand on the edge and suffer. "Nothing oh nothing on the earth can suffer like a woman young and all alone. " A thousand treasures that I wanted were lacking. I have a genius of a kind that has always been with me. I have an excellent strong young woman's body. A pitiably starved soul. With this equipment I have gone through the last two years. I am fraught with a poignant misery, the misery of nothingness. With no particulart thing to occupy me, I write everyday. Writing is a necessity like eating. I do a little housework and on the whole I am rather fond of parts of it. I like scrubbling floors, indeed I have gained much of my strenth and gracefulness of body from scrubbing the kitchen floor. To say nothing of some fine points of philosophy. It brings a certain energy to ones body and brain. Mostly though I take walks far away in the open country. I have reached some astonishing subtleties of conception as I have wlked for miles over the sand and barrenness. Among the little hills and gulches. Their utter desolateness is an inspiration to the long, long thoughts and to the nameless wanting. Everyday I walk over this desert. So my life then sems ordinary and comfortable to the average person. That as it may be to me is an empty damne weariness. I have not lacked listeners though these people do not appreciate me. I can see far, far inward. There is a finely drawn line between a genius and a fool.It is but a tiny step. Like between great and little, the tender and the contemptuous, the sublime and the ridiculous.

The aggressive and the humble, paradise and perdition. I have entered into certain things marvelously deep. I know things. It is magnificent of me to have gotten so far at the age of nineteen with no training other than that of the sand and barrenness. Magnificent do you hear? Very often I take this fact in my hand and squeeze it hard like an orange to get the sweet, sweet juice from it. I squeeze a great deal of juice from it every day, the juice is renewed like the VITALS OF PROMOTHEUS. I squeeze and squeeze and drink the juice to be satisfied. This is not a diary. It is a portrayal. It is my inner life shown in its nakendness. I am trying my utmost to show everything to reveal every petty vanity and weakness. Every phase of feeling, every desire. I probe my soul to its depths, to expose its shades and half lights.

There are feelings that rise and rush over me, overwhelmingly. I am helpless, crushed and defeated before them. It is as if they were written on the walls of my soul chamber in an unknown language. \tab My soul goes blindly seeking, seeking asking. Nothing answers. I cry out after some unknown thing with all the strength of my being. Every nerve and fibre in my young woman's soul reaches and strains in anguished unrest. At times as I hurry over my sadness and barrenness, all my lifes manifold passions culminate in utter rage and woe. Waves of intense, hopeless longing rush over me and envelope me round and round. I shall go mad, I shall go mad! I say over and over to myself. But no! No one goes mad. The devil does not propose to release anyone from so beautifully wrought, artistic damnation. He looks to it that ones senses are kept fully intact and he fastens to them with steel chains the Demon Of Unwrest. It hurts, oh it tortures me in the endles days! You know what Mary Maclane says here is how I feel at this present time. I don't mean to be negative but I suppose it's the deep artistic nature that I have and I will never shed. I don't know who to talk about it. Except of course Jesus. It drives me, I feel to write like it's my only means of sanity. Survival at this time.

The struggles of everyday life and the entailing responsibilities can be too much for some of us. Especially I believe in these brutal END TIMES. Let's all face it, it's not the 1950's! The curse fo mental illness is also an inherent blessing. Here is some more brilliant insight in te writings of Lara Jefferson. Miss Jefferson's writing whcih is magnificent, was written in the 1940's in the kind of disturbed psychiatric ward that isn't very common anymore in this day and age of institutions. This material is considered a minor psychiatric classic. I will put but a portion of it here. This by the way really speaks to me, perhaps it will to some of you! Quote; "I could not make the riffle of living according to the precepts and standards society demand of itself." "I find myself locked up with others of my kind in a hospital for the insane." "There is nothing wrong with me-except I was born at least two thousand years too late." Ladies of Amazonian proportions and berserker propensities have passed quite out of vogue an have no place in this too damned civilized world." Had I been born in the age and time when the world dealt in a straight-forward manner with misfits, why not meet the requirements of living? I would not have been much of a problem to my contemporaries. Because the poor deluded taxpayers of America insist on the delusion they are civilized, they strain themselves to the breaking point to keep institutions for over care in operation. Then when they break down under the strain of trying to live up to the standards they set for themselves. The officials who they have appointed for the office, pronounced them insane and they are committed to institutions. I know I cannot think straight but the conclusions I arrive at are very convincing to me and I still think the whole system is a regular Hades itself. There is nothing I can do about it, for I have been relieved of the responsibility of trying. It is just another of the vicious cycles that are forever whirling about our destinies.

"Here I sit even though I was once a so-called intelligent member of society. I must have had a fair share of intelligence or I could not have conducted myself according to the rules as long as I did. Now, I cannot conduct myself according to the rules set for me. Since something has broken loose within me and I am insane differing from these others to the extent that I still have sense enough to know it; which is a mark of spectacular intelligence, so they tell me.

"Here I sit, mad as a hatter with the choice of becoming more mad. Recover enough of my sanity to be allowed to go back to the life which drove me mad."If that is not a vicious circle, I hope I never encounter one.

Today the circle has stopped chasing itself long enough to drop me somewhere along the unmarked line between stark lunacy and harmless eccentricity. The latter is as near to normal as I ever hope to get.

With all of the study men of this calling have done to help abnormal people, nothing has been discovered which will enable them to reach into the dim caverns of a crooked brain and to make the crooked places straight. I want to state La here with what Lara has said that God said in HIS WORD that who can make the crooked paths and way straight? but I Jehovah? I AM HE WHO MAKES THE WATER IN YOUR DESERT.

Lara continurs to say, and I quote; "They have endless ideas and theories but when it comes down to actual performance of making an insane person sane they are helpless."

How true that is isn't it? I knew something that I the author knew. That something insidious and sinister was happening to me that I could not comprehend or cope with. Madness is like a cancer, it must be treated in time if the patient is to recover. That is precisely what Dr. Hoffer says of schizophrenia, as I have previously mentioned. \par

Life for anyone is an individual thing. For one who is insane, it is a naked and lonely thing.

I learned that in my days of raving. There are those who love me of whom I dare not think at all just now. To them death that has to do with shrouds and coffins would be preferable to the chaotic darkness. A pitiful creature who could not cope with life as she found it, nor could she escape it. Nor adjust herself to it. She was take to destruction and

God alone who knows all about inner emotions is the only one able to judge whether her end was a defeat or a triumph. There is nothing to stand on nothing beneath me but a vast treacherous quagmire of despondency, followed by periods of exultation and ecstasy. Neither condition has any foundation in logic. All my life I have been either in the throes of the one or the other. So have I.

If the weak, fearing creature as I have become then the world must have had her all wrong.

She was not an imbecile, but a genius.

She had come out of hell and had both the odor of smoke and scorched flesh upon her. So she has the audacity to look at the fate stretched before her and laugh as she sees it. She cares nothing at all for the things that her predecessors considered of valuse. She mocks at the shadow of her former person and waves a boLd flag of defiance.

This continue on of course but you may never find these lengthy and tedious. Yet note in both of these deep minded accounts and outlooks the startingly brilliance of them. The great depth of thought and understanding! Are these people really mad? Or are the ones OUTSIDE of these walls who considered themselves so normal and proper a more insidious kind of insanity? Like the poor deluded taxpayers of America insist on the delusion they are civilized! Lara was twenty nine when this torment began. I like what she says hare, it's rather beautfiul it caught me and swept me all the way through hell and very far into Heaven. She says as well "That thing that I feared the most has come upon me." (From Job in the Bible) She was not aware (Lara) that this verse came straight out of the Bible. My own mother always feared insanity. What I've noticed about both of these women, they were of scottish descents.

CHAPTER 18

My own family (on both sides) have a relatively good amount of scottish in us. There is no doubt, the "so called coincidences" are too numerous. The recurring instances of mental disease in places like Scotland and Ireland. In Ireland they have found a high level of COPPER in the soil. Copper in high levels is a malfunction connected with schizophrenia. Also speaking of countries pertaining to this Sweden has had the highest incidence of suicide for the longest time. Well, I'm all these; Irish, Scottish, and Swedish.

I guess that's three strikes against me?

CHAPTER 19

I must continue to add the writings of this Lara Jefferson, it's profound. This writing of the soul, I can totall relate to. It's really one of the keys to all this. Quote: "I became mad not because of some inner deformity but because of to close supervision and trying. Trying to force the thing into an unnatural mold. Perhaps this trouble is a result of too much here. I believe you've had a good taste of these two people. As I'm writing this a lovely sunshower is cascading dow. I think of many things when I read these women. I'm startled at the brilliance of them and the deep perception many people don't seem to have. From my own painful experiences, I have found the positive, sunny side the sunshower. Yes, the appreciation for simple life itself. I've always loved the beauty of nature. Oh and the heavenly touch of the cool breezes of each season. You are never the same again after being "Mad" afflicted. I know that even after the years passed I needed and still need consistent healing. Then would be flashbacks and memories that would stab with their unavoidable agony. As Dr, Hoffer said; "Schizophrenia leaves its indelible stamp. Then on the other hand the Lord can do things and make you over like no physicians can ever know about. As I was continuing to read Lara Jefferson's manuscript she talked of other women patients there (at the insane assylum) giving them appropriate names. One among the others was spitting and screaming, frothing at the mouth. She also said her eyes turned into something that wasn't human. That's clear to me that it is more than just psychoananlytical. It is obviously the forces of darkness, demons. Many missionaries, evangelists in their own servise had demon possessed people doing exactly that. Writhing on the floor like a snake with verbal profanity. My own brother saw it in a Christian meeting!

With the mentally ill I've perceived a transferring of spiritual awareness one to the other singing songs of Jesus then into ungodly utterances and swearing. So I truly believe that they have a more inate awareness of the spiritual realms than the average Joe. Again I'm speaking of the mentally ill. That is why it is a direct link with the underworld. First I believe the person is created with a "heightened" spiritual sense and as a child starts to show these different characteristics. Plus, eventually a heightened sensitivity in feelings and emotion can cause the delicate child alot of discomfort and pain. I was in a completely different world as a child. My mind was very rapid and I had total innocence. Right up to the age of fifteen. I thank God for when I grew up at a time when things weren't prematurely stuffed down the throats of children. When I was in school, the Lord's Prayer was still said every morning. Look how far it's gone now, right out the window.

CHAPTER 20

I want to put here a few Psalms of David regarding the afflicted.

PSALM 8; VERSE 9 onwards

THE LORD IS A STRONGHOD FOR THE OPPRESSED A STRONGHOLD IN TIMES OF TROUBLE . AND THOSE WHO KNOW THY NAME PUT THEIR TRUST IN THEE, FOR THOU O LORD HAS NOT FORSAKEN THOSE WHO SEEK THEE.
SING PRAISES TO THE LORD WHO DWELLS IN ZION!
TELL AMONG THE PEOPLES HIS DEEDS! FOR HE WHO AVENGES BLOOD IS MINDFUL OF THEM
HE DOES NOT FORGET THE CRY OF THE AFFLICTED.
BE GRACIOUS TO ME OH LORD! BEHOLD WHAT I SUFFER FROM THOSE WHO HATE ME, OH THOU

WHO LIFTETH ME UP FROM THE GATES OF DEATH; THAT I MAY ACCOUNT ALL THY PRAISES THAT IN THE GATES OF DEATH; THAT I MAY ACCOUND ALL THY PRAISES THAT IN THE GATES OF THE DAUGHTER OF ZION I MAY REJOICE IN THY DELIVERANCE.

PSALM 69 1-4

SAVE ME O GOD,
FOR THE WATERS HAVE COME UP TO MY NECK
I SINK IN THE MIRY DEPTHS
WHERE THERE IS NO FOOTHOLD
I HAVE COME INTO THE DEEP WATERS;
THE FLOODS ENGULF ME
I AM WORN OUT CALLING FOR HELP;
MY THROAT IS PARCHED
MY EYES FAIL
LOOKING FOR MY GOD
THOSE WHO HATE ME WITHOUT REASON
OUTNUMBER THE HAIRS OF MY HEAD;
MANY ARE MY ENEMIES
WITHOUT CAUSE,
THOSE WHO SEEK TO DESTROY ME.
I AM FORCED TO RESTORE WHAT I DID NOT STEAL.

VERSE 14-16

RESCUE ME FROM THE MIRE;
DO NOT LET ME SINK;
DELIVER ME FROM THOSE WHO HATE ME,

FROM THE DEEP WATERS
DO NOT LET THE FLOODWATERS ENGULF ME,
OR THE DEPTHS SWALLOW ME UP
OR THE PIT CLOSE ITS MOUTH OVER ME.
ANSWER ME, O LORD OUT OF THE GOODNESS OF
YOUR LOVE;
IN YOUR GREAT MERCY TURN TO ME.
DO NOT HIDE YOUR FACE FROM YOUR SERVANT;
ANSWER ME QUICKLY, FOR I AM IN TROUBLE.
COME NEAR AND RESCUE ME;
REDEEM ME BECAUSE FO MY FOES.
YOU KNOW HOW I AM SCORNED, DISGRACED
AND SHAMED;
ALL MY ENEMIES ARE BEFORE YOU
SCORN HAS BROKEN MY HEART AND HAS LEFT
ME HELPLESS;
I LOOKED FOR SYMPATHY, BUT THERE WAS
NONE,
FOR COMFORTERS BUT I FOUND NONE.

PSALM 68; VERSE 35

YOU ARE AWESOME O GOD IN YOUR SANCTUARY
THE GOD OF ISRAEL GIVES POWER AND
STRENGTH TO HIS PEOPLE
PRAISE BE TO GOD!

PSALM 10; ONWARDS

THE HAPLESS IS CRUSHED, SINKS DOWN AND
FALLS BY HIS MIGHT, HE THINKS IN HIS HEART;
GOD HAS FORGOTTEN HE HAS HIDDEN HIS FACE,

HE WILL NEVER SEE IT

ARISE O LORD; O GOD LIFT UP THY HAND; FORGET NOT THE AFFLICTED

WHY DOES THE WICKED RENOUNCE GOD AND SAY IN HIS HEART, THOU WILT NOT CALL INTO ACCOUNT?

THOU DOST SEE; YEA THOU DOST NOTE TROUBLE AND VEXATION, THAT THOU MAYEST TAKE IT INTO THY HANDS; THE HELPLESS COMMITS HIMSELF TO THEE; THOU HAST BEEN THE HELPER OF THE FATHERLESS

O LORD, THOU WILT HEAR THE DESIRE OF THE MEEK, THOU WILT STRENGTHEN THEIR HEART, THOU WILT INCLINE THY EAR TO DO JUSTICE TO THE OPPRESSED SO THAT MAN WHO IS OF THE EARTH MAY STRIKE TERROR NO MORE.

ALL WHO SEE ME MOCK AT ME, THEY MAKE MOUTHS AT ME THEY WAG THEIR HEADS; ALL WHO SEEM ME MOCK ME. HE COMMITTED HIS CAUSE TO THE LORD; LET HIM DELIVER HIM, LET HIM RESCUE HIM, FOR HE DELIGHTS IN HIM!

And verse 24 of Psalm 22

FOR HE HAS NOT DESPISED NOR ABHORRED THE AFFLICTION OF THE AFFLICTED; AND HE HAS NOT HID HIS FACE FROM HIM. O LORD, I BESEECH THEE, SAVE MY LIFE.

Verse 8

FOR THOU HAST DELIVERED MY SOUL FROM DEATH, MY EYES FROM TEARS MY FEET FROM STUMBLING; I WALK BEFORE THE LORD IN THE LAND OF THE LIVING. I KEPT MY FAITH, EVEN WHEN I SAID; \'cf AM GREATLY AFFLICTED. I SAID IN MY CONSTERNATION, MEN ARE ALL A VAIN HOPE.

THEN THERE'S FINALLY THE THANKSGIVING FOR DELIVERANCE.

Psalm 118 verse 5

OUT OF MY DISTRESS I CALLED ON THE LORD! THE LORD ANSWERED ME AND SET ME FREE. WITH THE LORD ON MY SIDE I DO NOT FEAR.

Verse 13
I WAS PUSHED HARD SO THAT I WAS FALLING BUT THE LORD HELPED ME.

THE LORD IS MY STRENGTH AND MY SONG HE WAS BECOME MY SALVATION

CHAPTER 21

I had a dream some years back of my mother and I at the house where I grew up the one I mentioned on McRae Ave. Anyway my mother was on the back steps of the deck, coming down the stairs. Out of our garage window flew a arrow, (which I saw in the spirit came from my grandmother) it lodged in my mother's lip and I could feel in my SOUL DEEPLY the pain and anguish it was causing my mother, and I felt it personally. We pulled it out together my mother and I. My mother and I were always there for each other, one of the strongest bonds I would ever have on this earth. Not everyone has such a deep close relationship with their mother which I would find out later. The corresponding scripture that seems to fit this dream is;

Psalm 11; 1-3

IN THE LORD I TAKE REFUGE; HOW CAN YOU SAY TO ME, "FLEE LIKE A BIRD TO THE MOUNTAINS, FOR

LO THE WICKED BEND THE BOW'THEY HAVE FITTED THEIR ARROW TO THE STRING, TO SHOOT IN THE DARK AT THE UPRIGHT IN HEART; IF THE FOUNDATIONS ARE DESTROYED WHAT CAN THE RIGHTEOUS DO?"

I mention this; to show that our worlds that we live in are more than just physical. I believe the interpretation of the dream is that; because I helped her take the arrow out, it was my souL link with hers. Having the same illnes, right after hers. We were both survivors. Vital instruments for each other. For many years after that. Still to this day. The arrow of course comes from satan. It's piercing of the lip and I forgot to mention, the forehead is very significant. For schizophrenia is of "The Mind" and of the tongue. Like is stated before; \ 'c4 Battle For The Mind And Soul. Why not the arrow in the heart or up to other parts of the body? This is why I believe; Note in the third verse of this psalm, If the foundations are destroyed what can the righteous do? FOUNDATIONS, that can mean family life, the basic institute that makes up society and part of your foundation as a human being is your MIND. Well this did crumble in our lives probably because of more than one ARROW. The meaning for the righteous for us would be that the Lord knows who will become His righteousness. So satan will attack beforehand to prevent that. I want to put a few more psalms here, to show how God cares for the afflicted. I believe He has a special love for them. Here's Psalm 22;6 This is how the mentally ill feel sometimes.

"BUT I AM A WORM AND NO MAN; SCORNED BY MEN AND DESPISED BY THE PEOPLE."

ALL WHO SEE ME MOCK AT ME; THEY MAKE MOUTHS AT ME THEY WAG THEIR HEADS; ALL WHO SEE ME MOCK AT ME. HE COMMITTED HIS CAUSE TO THE LORD; LET HIM DELIVER HIM, LET HIM RESCUE I, FOR HE DELIGHTS IN HIM!

And Verse 24 of Psalm 22

FOR HE HAS NOT DESPISED NOR ABHORRED THE AFFLICTION OF THE AFFLICTED; AND HE HAS NOT HID HIS FACE FROM HIM. O LORD, I BESEECH THEE SAVE MY LIFE.

Psalm 118 verse 5

OUT OF MY DISTRESS I CALLED ON THE LORD! THE LORD ANSWERED ME AND SET ME FREE. WITH THE LORD ON MY SIDE I DO NOT FEAR

Verse 13

I WAS PUSHED HARD SO THAT I WAS FALLING BUT THE LORD HELPED ME. THE LORD IS MY STRENGTH AND MY SONG. HE HAS BECOME MY SALVATION.

GOD HAS NOT GIVEN US THE SPIRIT OF FEAR BUT OF POWER OF LOVE AND A "SOUND MIND"

A DOUBLE MINDED IS UNSTABLE IN ALLS HIS WAYS

SEDUCING SPIRITS BEGUILING "UNSTABLE SOULS"

FOR WE WRESTLE NOT WITH FLESH AND BLOOD BUT WITH POWERS OF THE AIR PRINCIPALITIES, WICKEDNESS IN HIGH PLACES STRONGHOLDS.

NOT BY MIGHT NOT BY POWER BUT BY MY SPIRIT SAYS THE LORD…

CHAPTER 22

Finally on schizophrenia, from a normal secular point of view, it is important to seek the purpose and intentions around which (insanity) or should I say cruel affliction, is organized. One thing I haven't mentioned is there are varying levels of illness of this sort. Also various levels of well, insanity. Different contributing factors and we must never forget the very physical aspect of it as well. The mind and spirit. When I was addressing earlier on of the conversion of the hormone adrenaline into adrenochrome in schizophrenia. Well the doctors have found som similar substances which were in people who were just physically ill. So of course this additional evidence that schizophrenics are physically ill as well. It goes deeply into scientific and biochemical factors. The brain itself has been found to use an enormous amount of energy.

There is a comprehensive theory of schizophrenia, which is quite interesting. Here is the summary;

1. Due to chromosomes, which contain genes derived from parents, the person used normal chemicals in an abnormal way.

2. As a result at a certain time in life toxic chemicals are produced in the body which interfere with the normal operations of body and brain.

3. Therefore the world and the body as experienced by all the senses appears to be altered-strange, different, unreal etc.

4. But the person has learned to accept the evidence of the senses as real or true and continues to do so. He or she is unaware that the changes in their perceptions are due to changes in their brain. They believe that it is the external world which is altered.

5. He reacts in a way he considers appropriate, but as the perceptions are inappropriate, so must be his actions. As judged by others in similar ways.

6. His total behaviour, personality etc is therefore different and this brings into play a host of social consequences in family, friends and last of all society as a whole.

7. This results in actions by society which may place him in hospital, jail or banish him to a neighbouring counry.

All of the above takes into play perceptual changes which in turn is caused by the chemical changes in the body, affecting the brain.

It makes me think of just how one merciful touch of Jesus's

hand the Great Physician could reavert and heal all of that. There is a very interesting test that is done with the perceptual changes. It is called the HOD test. It's based to a large degree on this change of perception. It has 145 cards and patient are asked to sort these into true and false piles. If the subject is significantly high in the score regarding opposite perception, then they are probably ill.

As I have said before the brain itself has been found to use an enormous amount of energy. The HOD test that I just previously stated was developed by the authors in 1961'on the basis of differences they had observed between people who had the illness and those who did not.

Here is an interesting account of a former patient who experienced a "VISIONARY" state, He said the HAND OF HIS ENEMY DESCENDED UPON HIS ARM WHICH CAUSED HIS HAND TO BECOME WHITE. HIS BRAIN OPENED AND A MESSAGE WAS TAPPED OUT BY HIS ENEMY, WHICH WAS SLANDEROUS AND THREATENING. He of course became frightened, left his farm and moved to a hotel where he lived for eight months. This before hospital admission. It has an obvious aupernatural taste to it. As does this one of a fifty one year old woman who came to hospital in reponse to a voice which told her to. A voice which told her to? Many accounts of people who were told by "voices" to either kill or go to a particular place (sometimes a different country) are simply looked upon by the media as mentally ill, imbalanced or criminally insane. Yes, they may be but who's the greatest author on insanity? Aren't there demons for various vices that are commissioned by satan to whisper to people? To commit terrible acts of violence. The scripture states that He was a murderer from the beginning. He has come to steal, kill and destroy. I think you could put a little more meaning to thieves with that! Not that all thieves are whispered to by spirits. For some of them it's their own wills and inner choice of sinfulness. But I think more Christians have to have an open mind and keep things in a discerned balance. Think about that scripture, I wrote pages back, "We wrestle not against flesh and blood, but against principalities, spirits wickedness in high places. High places can imply a lot as well if you think carefully about it.

Getting back to that fifty one year old woman, she then had visual hallucinations; a mouse which seemed to say JUDAS to her! It was apparently moving on the curtains. The first thing that came to mind was of course Judas who betrayed Christ. I mean it didn't say Peter, Frank or even a disciples name. Judas… I will leave this as it is without my other thoughts on this matter. Like I said of people that are ill, I've met or read about and from my own first hand experience. I am thoroughly convinced of these people being interactive with the spiritual realm. I think that's why what they say or experience seem bizarre to the rest of the world. Plus there is something about the distorting and opening of the mind that doesn't and can't just create an empty vacuum, void of some kind of spiritual action. Something has to happen. Like a preacher I remember once said, there isn't once square inch on this world that isn't claimed by God and counter-claimed by satan. These people most of them as far as I know are also very sensitive. You have to be to partake of these world. It's a "HEIGHTENED AWARENESS" Like the Holy Spirit is gentle and powerful at the same time. As I was speaking about hallucinations, that may be more than they seem; there was also a case I came across that briefly states how a young woman had apparently seen Jesus. He said she was destined to be "HIS BRIDE", she then quit her job, secluded herself in reading the Bible. I personally have no problem in believing that she really saw "The Son Of God." Indeed saying those words. It seems over and over that there is an opening to the reality of spiritual realms that happens with this distorting of the mind and perceptions. Schizophrenia has much to do with perceptions, such as smell, touch time itself. All of this of course affecting thought. We se the world around us as all there is. The world here and now is all period, to the unbeliever. But we as christians know there is another, unseen by the naked eye. In fact we know thee are beings swirling around us, invisible. So to change our unseeing eye, we would have to have our senses altered and our perceptions as well. Makes sense doesn't it?

This came to me like a revelation, yet it's really quite simple and sane. So I truly believe they are not just hallucinating things that are not there. They are entering into that unseen world for real. Yes, really seeing things that are there. Entering into that unseen world for real. Entering into that unseen world that can only be gazed upon by "street drugs" which is also a BIG TIME altering of the senses. That's THE KEY, THE ALTERING OF ALL FOUR SENSE. As previously documented. Think about it carefully and judge for yourself. Remember, too like the Lord said; that it was "demonically inherited." Yes it's biochemical and that imbalance of biochemistry alters the whole human psyche and tears down the veil from the eyes. For we are not just body and mind, but body, mind and spirit. One affects the other. We all start to learn that eventually. The body ailments affect the brain patterns in schizophrenia and I believe the sensitivity of the soul. Yet the psychologist and biochemists just stop at the brain, if they only knew how real the spirit is.

I mean for heaven's sake none of us would be alive if it wasn't for the existence within our mortal bodies of our souls. Thinking of some scriptures correlating with other aspects of the disease for depression a Biggy for this illness. The Word Of God says; "Sorrow drieth up the bones, but a merry heart maketh a cheerful countenance." One of my favourites is "The Joy Of The Lord Is My Strength." Note it says it's my strength, so obviously sadness has a weakening affect on an individual. I believe you can interpret "Drying up" of the bones like a disease. What happens when you are weakened? Your resistance is lowered and you are much more susceptible to illnesses. With schizophrenia the chemicals and hormones are being used in an abnormal way. When stress comes it starts the chain reaction of events and the beginning stages of the illness. Schizophrenia causes great fatigue. Very often it is the first symptom to appear. It comes on slowly and insidiously and is very disabling. Oh do remember that well! That was a prominent thing for me. I could sleep for days. You really suffer with that. I mean nobody in their right mind wants to sleep their life away and when you are chemically exhausted, forced to do things it's painful. i used to have naps with my feet facing toward the head and my head positioned at the end of the bed. The reverse of what is normally done. I knew years later this was strange, but did't think much about it. Not until I saw a movie on schizophrenia. The actress playing the lead role was Nancy Mckeon. In the picture she did the very same thing. It had a subtle, yet striking affect on me. Realizing the common thread of the symptoms, I was told I was lazy and copping out in one school that I went to. It was because I had to take periodic naps. This is common, other ill persons have the same difficulty with an ignorant society. One young man I came across in my research was only twenty-six and he had seventeen years of chronic fatigue. A hideously long duration, too long. When he started on nicotinic acid (Another name for niacin) the exhaustion still remained with him for one year with this treatment. But now he found he was able to grasp his course of studies with little difficulty. No, he was not stupid, but very ill.

Here I want to continue on with some more info from resources. The social factors of this illness follow naturally from the perceptual and the other disturbances which accompany it. It can mean rejection through the misinterpreting of the other persons actions. Two people as they walk toward one another are at first too far away for recognition to be possible. When they get closer, it may seem that up to this point nothing could possibly go wrong. Yet much can and does go wrong when the schizophrenic is involved. As people walk toward us, we see them getting closer. They also become bigger and bigger. We learn to interpret this enlarging of the image on the eye retina as meaning the individual is getting close, yet it may equally mean that the object from which the light was being reflected was getting larger. This is a subtle distinction which schizophrenic patients are sometimes unable to make. Many of them have reported the eerie and frightening experience of a tiny dwarf becoming a huge and menacing giant as it looms forward.

In normal people, by some complex and not yet understood mechanisms of the brain, the approaching figure remais roughly the same size. But for many schizophrenics we know this reassuring mechanism goes wrong. Driving a car is very difficult because timing is off balance. On coming cars seems to rush by too quickly. In

addition, they are uncertain of their position in their own car lane. They may feel they are too close to the center line or to the edge. Due to these perceptual difficulties and lack of energy, the schizophrenic person cannot respond to those around him, either as quickly or as consistently as normals can. I've been stating here numerous times, as "Normals can" but the the incredible thing is that after schizophrenia is healed the person can become more normal and as I said before, healthier than those who have never been sick with this. You go from such a debilitating state of body, mind and soul to sometimes outstanding fitness in one of these areas or all three. I personally can do physical things with speed and dexterity, yet I still get extrememly exhausted. Sometimes so tired from the simplest things that don't tire someone else. Yes there are still those who doubt that this disease is physically inherited and above all that it is "demonically inherited." Being very physical, that is the vulnerable ground for the spirits. I believe they obviously have failed to recognize that the disease occurs in over 10% of the human race. These skeptics have never explained why an illness often thought to be due to an unfitness of its' sufferers for the full rigours of life, should occur in so many people. I've talked about the physical infirmities of this, but there are also highly interesting advantages it confers on its victims. Schizophrenics ahve an extraordinary tolerance for injected histamine. Schizophrenic soldiers have a very low incidence of allergies compared with similar young soldiers woho have head injuries.

Rheumatoid arthritis is a very infrequent occurrence as well. Studies also suggest that they are not as likely to suffer shock after catastrophies, such as perforation of an internal organ, or a coronary thrombosis. Inquiries show that they

Read

are highly resistant to wound and surgical shock after grave injuries and burns.

This superiority may seem a high price to pay for a tendency to a disese such as this, but for some people it may be of vital importance to survival. Like many schizophrenics, he might well survive misfortune whcih would kill his fellows. His perceptual difficulties or even frank hallucinations, may cause him little or no distress.

A close look at history shows that those whose perceptions ranged from the unusual to the bizarre have from time to time had great influence. In the arts, music politics, philosophy, religion and science. This greatly alters not only the viewpoint but the actions of our whole species. That's why I said these valuable and frequently misunderstood individuals must be spared for the enrichment of mankins, for their kind of minds they have with the great gifts and insights they can share. Yes, to make life more of a blessing for the rest who toil and labor in the city offices, or the sick dying and lonely, confined to hospitals. For the coming generations to leave them with something tangible that hopefully will lead them to God, our Creator.

Schizophrenia then appears to be beneficial as well as harmful to the individual and to the species. If properly understoo, can be useful to men. It has life saving qualities with which it seems to be associated. It is very important to be compassionate to these ill people. The age old adage of doing the sick no harm should still be held in front today. Mentally ill people are very sensitive people, like I have said before they take things very much to heart. So of course our concern should be of understanding the illness with an empathy and a sympathy which contrasts sharply with the psychiatrist's aim of destroying it and changing it into something else. Just as stated before, some kind of appreciation of the "value" of the illness seems indicated. In this regard the words of the philosopher, Santayana in his 'Dialogues In Limbo' may be of use here. The physician knows madness in one way, he collects the symptoms of it. The causes and the glory of the illusion, which after all are the madness itself, are open only to the madman or to some sympathetic spirit as prone to madness as he is. The patient's intimate connection with what he is describing, can also be said to have a special interest in the proceeddings. His ignorance of psychiatric theory may permit him to formualte novel conclusions which lie outside the usual framework. Strangely enough the amateur psychiatry of these patients on the whole does not sound at all bad to the psychiatric ear. Yes, a high degree of sophistication is frequently found where it seems to ahve no right to be and there is an astounding "high proportion" of insights which border on significant psychiatric advances. So one is led to speculate that "patient psychiatry" might make a meaningful contribution to the understanding of mental illness. Yes, I believe in environmental stress contribution to the orderly and normal functioning of the biological integrity and the organism. From the 'Phenomenology Of Mind' literature has termed the abnormal as not disruption and disorientation but rather an entering to a superior chain of reality. With few exception the ill themselves embrace their illnesses and identify with them. Although there is an obvious suffering with them, there is also gratification, excitement and meaning. Even when the illness is over, it is often viewed positively. I have not been able to not do this with my experience.

To "so called" saner minds it may seem completely

incomprehensible that psychosis with its attendant suffering, humiliation and alienation, should if genuine freedom of choice exist, win the day over a normality. That not only carries a variety of material advantages with it, but is also endowed with legitimacy and moral rectitude. Through his psychosis, the person renounces what is normally regarded as perhaps the most valuable and significant of all life's activities, participation in a social group and the possibility of positive relationships with other people. Yet the rewards of normality are probably overestimated and for many may be seen only with difficulty. For the person immersed in a particularily difficult or unrewarding life situation, it may seem that almost any alternative will have more to offer. Our image of individuals weighing in the balance, the various goods that are offered by a spectrum of action the carefully rationally choosing of the weightiest goods. This is most certainly an incorrect hypothesis. The perversity of human beings is such that they break the rules simply to assert theier freedom. One of the features of the mentally ill is that they are opposed to a normality which is intimately related to the major value orientation of "western society." It may be asserted therefore that abnormality involves a "negative relationship" to prevailing social normative prescriptions, perhaps the most extreme and complete form of negation that is possible. There is revealed a "CORE" of rebellion and rejection of expectations regarding social participation. This has termed as \ 'e4lienation. In this association of abnormality with a refusal to be bound by things as they are and with the striving to be different, we have what is at bottom a concern with the category of change and transcedence. It is a call to be different. A way to experience life in a sense richer to the so called normality that proceeded the illness, nor a negations of the illness. The "New State" must rather involve a genuine moving to a new solution, a movement which would have been impossible without the illness. Thus a quotation from what I wrote down previously of Lara Jefferson, \ 'cf cannot escape from the madness by the door I came in, that is certain, nor do I want to." This provides a vivid living image of psychopathology, not always the useual one it is treu, but one which carries the 'conviction of reality.'

As I have said before of these particular people being the ones who seem to pertain to the other "WORLD" much more.

I have a very interesting experience of Lara Jefferson; she was suddenly free on a lake in her (so called imagination)she states that it was not imagination but something more peculiar. For she said that mere imagination cannot transport a person tied down, (she was in a strait jacket at the time) in an insane assylum to set them free in some far away place. She so vividly found herself on a pebbled beach at dawn, feeling the chilly morning air around her, the dip of cars and hear the squeak of locks and the ripple of water against a boat.

She continues on with a beautiful description of the scenery around her. It is written in a delightfully poetic way. She said it was so poignant and perfect, scintillating her dull sensed organs so that it must be an ecstasy. You know my readers, some well known Catholic saints had very realistic ecstasies and further. To spiritual phenomenon, such as bilation. Which is truly having their 'souls representation' in a different place while their bodies are still in another. I mea, they were in two different places by documented eye witnesses. This has been thoroughly investigate and verified over an extensive period of time by the Catholic church's authorities. Many of you I know reading this will not believe it. Or perhaps you will. I realize this, but those of you who are well versed Catholices, know about these well known Holy people. You have no problem with it. They weren't occultic, witches warlocks or anything of that nature. God can do exactly what He chooses, I don't think enough people realize that. I mean we want to experience or read about true incidences of the supernatural, then when it's there we are "The skeptics." Human nature eh? So sad. So Lara's ecstasy which may have been more in a real world then we'll ever know is called a "Delusion" by the psychiatrists and of course good old society. She continues on here with such fine wisdom, that I must share it with you. She said she had such rest and freedom in the floating current of her thoughts without the struggle of forcing her thinking to continue in the channels she had been taught were right. All the things she had strived for during a whole lifetime of fierce wanting, fell so far away from her that she did not know that she had ever suffered or feared. I love this here; I can relate to it so well. She says that singing is the natural spontaneous expression of freedom. She sang song after song in that insane assylum, she was in a true sense of the word, "FREE" Nothing mattered. Later on in that sme instance of experience she has more so-called delusions as her nerves snap. She sees a great bat flitting in and out behind the radiator, then in the corner of her room she sees a creature about two feet tall, jumping up and down. He was laughing. Now to me bats and small creatures that laugh at your torture are evil…Bats have always ben asssociated with evil, the vampires in movies etc. I have know of a woman who through a difficult period of her life had a creature in the corner of her room eating raw meat, that was obviously an apparition of a real demon. What better place for bats and demons to show up than an insane assylum? There we have the "Battle For The Mind" again spiritual warfare. After all her torment she has her bath, that as she beautifully puts it wa perhaps a "Baptism" for she felt cleansed and pure. Her soul exalted within her. Here in regards to psychosis is a terrific quotation from William James; "For aught we know to the contrary, 103'or 104'fahrenheit might be much more favourable temperature for truths to germinate and sprout in than the more ordinary bloodheat of 97 or 98'degrees."

I can see more and more of depression, mental illness and schizophrenia to be coming out of the forced darkness it has been put in. More endeavours to bring information and clearer understanding to the public and society at large. I believe from how I personally have felt inside all my life and by confirming this by talking to someone with similiar ways that certain people definitely have an extremely "Heightened Awareness" I know for a fact that it's a minority in the majority. On top of that when you become a christian it becomes even more acute. For now you have the spiritual realms revealed to you, thus you enter into it. I know for myself and others like me, that life is more difficult and stressfull. For we're aware of all around us more than the average Joe. Yet at the same time it can be richer and more beautiful. The usual pros' and cons of the laws of the universe so to speak. That spark! That vibrancy! This seems to be seriously lacking in the rest of humanity. Oh yes, they have their spark but usually through artificial means and also through believing a lie or lies. This is precisely what the Bible speaks about when it says that "They would have their eyes blinded, their ears deafened or stopped lest they should hear the "Light of the Glorious Gospel." Then be made free. Who the Son sets free is free indeed. True freedom of all of you. Your enlightened nature and personality of ultimately your "soul." It's hard to accept a fragile and often torturous make-up or you may prefer 'psyche' There's usually a built in prerequisite of certain individuals that mark them as prime candidates for this dreadful affliction. Like I have stated in a earlier chapter they are usually the musicians, the painters, dancers writers poets and teachers. All of the creative arts, then it ripples into politicians, mathematicians, (John Nash) lawyers. The bottom line? Brilliant, intellectual people. Is this an accident? I think not. It's been over thirty years since I was so deathly ill ad at death's door. Yet I still bear the complex and delicate violin strings of my being. I still suffer tremendously from it, but that's really not a big issue to me anymore. For I am an extremely honed and strong soldier, WARRIOR. Which is what Louise means "Battle Maiden!" I find I have to know what I can and cannot do. Not to be pressured or controlled by anyone to do those things I have a "check" on. This takes alot of honour, courage and determination. What I was not created to do, but to be fairly fearless, like a racing human torch to that I have great skill and talent in. This is the fulfilling of DESTINY. If we were all in "tune" this way we would probably be slotted in better holes of the puzzle of our lives. Just the right shape of the piece fits in, otherwise someone with a chisel comes to shave us down to be forced into that shape. Yet it was not natural so it's like living a false deception, a very twisted puzzle! I just want to put in here the responsibilities of the community. The community may not thins its' responsible in this regard at all but it has responsibilites no less vital than the patients and their families. Unfortunately they do not often realize it. It is said that no community is stronger than its weakest link. The effects of illness in one individual involve others in ever widening circles. Until everyone is "directly" or \'efndirectly enmeshed.

Whole systems have to pick up the pieces after sick members in our comunities. Think about it; jails, police courts, welfare agencies including social aid; heavily staffed civil servant organizations and private organizations some of which are effective in planning their programs to encourage cure and rehabilitation. Some of which are ineffective in ignoring causes and treatment. The definite trend seems to shift the responsibility of treatment to the community, because psychiatrists do no know how to cure the mentally il. Better treatment would result in less time spent in hospital and less suffering and shame. It would make rehabilitation less essential, thus reducing the demands on the community.

CHAPTER 23

HERE IS A LIST OF THE RESPONSIBILITIES OF THE COMMUNITY AS I SEE IT;

1. Provide adequate hospitals that have a "Humanitarian Psychology" Not the structure (literally of the building) of an institution.

2. Staff them with competent psychiatrists knowledgable in orthomolecular nutrition, who also firmly believe in it.

3. Encourage, even demand effective merciful treatment of the mentally ill.

4. Accept them back as soon as they are ready into the mainstream of society. Without attaching any stigma to them and help to rehabilitate them by providing jobs and homes.

5. Above all support research which will give us answers to enigmatic questions.

6. When this is done there will be a noticeable reduction in the efforts we must now make. The money we now spend to endure sick people who have not been helped.

CHAPTER 24

I want to of course add that knowledge and information to enlightened minds about the "demonic" nature of this illness is extremely vital. This is why I have written this book. Yet even now those who are not yet Christians can hear of this side rather blatantly. It's a great witness to the reality of the "Spiritual" realm and to the glory of Jesus Christ in the deliverance. Some indeed are healed only by the medical realm and good nutrition. With careful monitoring of individual biochemistry to the synthetic drugs. Of course I'm speaking of paxell, haldol, risperidol etc. Then again, these should not, I repeat not be prologed. Since the damage to the vital organs, memory, performance etc, is not only altered but can have permanent consequences. Such as tardive dysknesia and brain atrophy. The aforementioned of course is the tremors, uncontrollable shaking of the hands, the legs with varying facial ticks, twitches etc.

So what about those who are not cured by these conventional medical means? or those who seem well for awhile then become ill again? Perhaps undealt with spirits? Then we have that "REVELATION" I previously wrote of "Pigs In The Parlour" The Lord showing where schizophrenia really comes from. How can anyone except an atheistic skeptic dispute that? For once regarding "The attitude" and treatment of these ill persons, I am lividly furious! Now looking back and still what I'm experiencing in the treatment of the gentle, weaker people is a cruel, less than human energy. A destructive energy originating from the "CORE" of a selfishly materialistic society. World at large. This energy of course spiritually dark in essence must be brought to a revelation truly to our Creator. The gentle, spiritual impressionistic souls are "THE REMNANT OF EDEN" So after the Biblical fall the virtues of these rightful qualities fell. They were replaced with these dark, opposing luciferic energies and drives. I have personally experienced "The mind" and spirit of destruction, that still desires and tries to destroy me. I must fight daily as we all do whether we know it or not, A Battle of man's nature and the powers and principalities of evil. So much of trials, spiritual warfare to this day has tried to chip away at my soundness, sanity of mind.

All the great composers, artists experienced this same feeling of a fight, outside and within. That fine line whether or not over the edge. A quivering tight-rope caught between one world and the next one. Which we are not supposed to step into without protection. Only as a christian with the Blood Of The Lamb can we combat tread into the enemy's territory. I know for certain that the Lord is readily on the side of the weak, "The poor in spirit" The broken afflicted ones and of course those that are inclined to be humble. For the scripture says He resisteth the proud and giveth grace to the humble. For the scripture says 'He resisteth the proud and giveth grace to the humble. He will bring down the proud and lofty and exalt the humble and meek. Blessed is the poor in spirit for theirs is the Kingdom Of God. Blessed are the meek for they shall inherit the earth. Blessed are the pure in heart for they shall see God. The most down trodden and despised of the world come into where I labor. As I'm writing this in Vancouver, B.C. I see the prostitutes, drunkards, homosexuals insane, poverty stricken. All colors, all walks of life. As I volunteer, I have never been in a nicer place. I'll tell you honestly the broken-spirited and humble people who are so ready to smile, receive assistance go a long way with me. I know they do with Jesus. Bless His name! For you see these are such of "The KIngdom Of Heaven." I just bet there will be a majority of these people up there. Sadly I say in these End Times you do not seem to meet many pure hearts anymore. Most people even the "Best" seem to have a selfish "Hidden Agenda" I observe that the abused have more of this at least a glimmer of this attribute. The more I work there the more \ 'f6ut of touch with the big city I become.

I like all women love to wear nice polished clothes and I can always have a myriad of them. Yet I really do like being rather inconspicuous in jogging pants and a long loose shirt or jeans. I've never liked being stared at much. I mean I can get my 5'8" blonde self all dolled up, but I'm on edge then. I suppose we all are rather transformed coming out of our teen years. So should it be.

I had quite an incredible dream while living in Victoria. It was in regards to the "Least Of These" being the largest occupats in heaven.

I was on a bus bench i the city, when several of the street

people were around me and one was laying jewels, trinkets of various shapes and value. Then an extremely thin man sat down beseide me and quoted scripture. I could literally smell the odor of his dirt jacket, it was so real. It was an eerie dark kind of twilight sky with a corresponding atmosphere. Definite symbolism there if you ask me. I've been gradually piecing it together. My dreams have ben extremely profound ever since I was a small child. God has definitely given me "A step in sleep" to the other world. Sometimes it shows like a revelation what is actually happening in the here and now. In the spiritual aspect of it. What comes to mind is the scripture; The Lord has poured upon you the spirit of deep sleep, to cover the seers and prophets. And the vision for you would be a vision for many. I certainly have very deep sleep.

You know the brain is an amazing creation, just as I have spokenof regarding the chemicals, hormones that are out of balance. A prevalent factor in schizophrenia and most mental illnesses.

It's so peculiar you know, there's many things I can do very well perhaps even exceptionally. Then other things just an ordinary degree. Or reading and following the instructions on a microwave dinner or some other food, I seem to have to read over and over out loud, and I go blank for a few minutes. LIke strange, yet high tech stuff etc, I'm fast and up there. Parts of the brain. My husband is very good for me because he is a man of practical action. I really need that, I, on the other hand depending on what it is, can analyze to death. Or go into what some people find is irritating detail when discussing something. Then the verbal friends I have that are similiar to me love it! So there we have it!! Fascinating…

How paradoxical is the make-up of people who become a candidate for mental illness. On one hand they are the outstanding world achievers, the famous actors, musicians of the past and present eras. Then some things of life that are not an issue in any way to the rest of society pushes them over the edge. I come from highly intellectual, yet nervous ancestors. Part of the package I suppose.

I have lived an exciting other worldly, but earth shattering life. Sometimes I'm in awe at how I've survived. Except of course for the Grace Of God!

A life my husband say most people, especially women couldn't live through at all. I mean what a contradiction, what an "unearthly paradox." I become tense when dealing with the public. You're in a sense a servant, like being an artist. Yet, I've experienced first hand that the world treats us more like unpaid bond-slaves. Trying to escape from the grip of the Pharaoh's dragging our bloody bodies over to the Promised Land. Oh and our weary Egyptian souls. We desire to serve on different terms and levels. Justice rules.

Like the Matrix movies says; "To realize that we are born into bondage, a prison for our minds that's been put on us."

I've felt ashamed ridiculous in revealing my seeming inadequacies in some basic coping skills. Yet again, the awesome PARADOX of doing mind blowing achievements with greater skill than others. Whoa!

Free your mind, let it all go, fear unbelief. I guess we are the unworldly misfits!

There's one world in which no matter how much work is involved, the pressure etc, I feel completely comfortable with. That's the stage for singing, playing the piano, dance, all the fine arts. Then acting, (for I've been able by the grace of God to achieve) for I've also been a young acting director.

Ah yes, and behind the Almighty pen to the paper. I've written songs and poetry since I was a small child. It comes naturally. I say that with as much humility and awe as I can. For I know where my talents come from and WHO I AM INDEBTED TO. It's an awesome thing to have the raw talent from God, then the technical, professional training to "hone" it. That's sometimes where we coing the terminology of "amateur" to "professional." At times charming virtues can be temporarily lost with professional training. On some occasions, like a lot more of life than we give attention to is the "Danger Of Generalizion" That's where a lot of people can and do get hurt. As I've previously mentioned the psychiatric realm is one of the most delicate tight rope in ths regard. For the individual biochemistry and personality is crucified by the will of the Caesar's of psychiatry. So much is changing in our world. Above all God wants needs more talented and committed people. Forgive the pun committed to Him not just institutionalized and labelled. To be the fully integrated people that the world desperately needs regardless of it's awareness. To set the captives free. What could be more of an imprisonment than the bondage of mental illness? I often wondered why the Lord would use such a wimpy person like me so very frail in some ways, yet very sensitive to do as He's spoken in "prophecy" such large, compelling things. I personally believe that the instances of "Miracles" are not such a rare occurrence as we are lead to believe. The dictionary meaning of a MIRACLE says "Something that defies the ability of the natural realm to achieve." Yet, many of us are "walking miracles" are we not? The more we tell the world around us of this truth, the better. God says He uses the weak and debase things of the world to confound the wisdom of men. It's quite oftent the child, or the beggar and

the mentally ill that will say the profoundes
more desperate you are the more you lo
assistance to the sky. For mankind as an unca
disappointing, betraying their fellow man. Tha
in the Bible states in a time of his dilemna and questioning
periods that he conferred not with flesha dn blood. Mental
illness, particularily "schizophrenia" causes the most
crucifying mental, spiritual and physical suffering of any of
the illnesses on the earth that we know. On the positive side
this can create such a spiritual and humanitarian awareness.
Which I've seen the most dramatic manifestations of. It
definitely connects to the clairvoyant, psychic realm.

Joan of Arc in the category of "Catholicism" was
considered a Great Mystic, saying she saw the Great
Archangel Michael and was instructed by him to the victory
of her country in France. On the other category of natural,
psychological fields she had been labelled a heretic and out
right schizophrenic! The awake visions she had of the
Archangel, Michael were explained as hallucinations in the
almighty realm of psychiatry. Especially Sigmund Freud
who felt he had the answers of most "neurosies" in sexual
repression, combined with cold clinical studies. If Freud's
nanny that was assigned to him had remained, I think
history in his regard would have been different. For she was
Catholic and he was studying the Bible, quite happy and
there was security. When she was taken away for false
suspicion of a bogus crime, history tells of the downward
slide. For Freud at still a tender age has to leave his home with
his father losing his occupation and poverty comes as a shock
to the family. At school a very atheistic tutor of Jewish
descent becomes the rapid replacement to the child Freud.
Almost immediately an alternative to the "Belief system" is

replaced with out right atheism and scientific evidence for all of life. The course of psychotherapy would then be almost forever tainted with this brick of psychiatric foundation. Through decades slowly chipping away with the chisel of inadequacy, ruined lives and treadmill zombies of the new age of neuroleptics, would this creed finally erode!

Before I could put my little toe into the experiences of the world, I was crucified unto the fulfillment of the Lord with schizophrneia. Mind you it has not been the only way of the cross, though I thought this was sufficient. Apparently the Lord chooses His ultimate place of "Ascension" knowing if you're the kind that can go through even more. We also know all these trials, life experiences can and have the potential for a broad span of ministry and of course empathy. Biochemical, psychological knowledge must never ever be disconnected from the "Mercy seat."

The basic humanitarian acknowledgement that all life has entwined into the very fibres of its' matrix. Some \'ebnigmas only need a deeper glance into the mirrored waters of thought and feeling. I have mostly run my life on the thread of emotions, eventually finding it turned into a rope that almost choked me to death. A fusion of feeling, analysis, soldier like will with the attributes of sensitivity, etc. helped me or should I say, gave me the skills to survive the upcoming auswitches wars and other battles I would face. The more you go through the wider the spectrum of those you can reach, bit by bit, here a little there a little. From Mother Theresa to the President. A servant to the Leader of many nations. The bigger the vision, the bigger the possibilities! We try to put God in a box and I'm sorry the shoe doesn't fit! We need to perceive the "symbolism" of the moment. Pick it up and at times RUN with it.

When we reject one another, because we are made in the image of God we are not only rejecting ourselves we are in essence rejecting part of God HIMSELF. If we can have a fraction of that in our minds, then of course we would view and treat each other alot differently. That's why the atheistic view is so destructive. No God, thus nothing with a Divine Imprint. No divinity, no responsibility of the created to the Creator. For hey, he doesn't exist. The evolutionist theory has the upper hand and governs all. That is what some people still believe. Unenlightened, we are not in any position no matter how prominent our status to reject anyone. Especially on a first meeting. God's word says that Man looks on the outward appearance, but God looks at the HEARTS. Bingo. Unfortunately those who do not have the required prerequisites of a harsh system end up as victims. The vulnerable captives of the Napoleons in power. So much shameful persecutions. One of the most vulnerable of society, next to the elderly and children is the "Mentally ill." THIS INFURIATES ME TO NO END! Cruelty has always abhorred me. To me first hand judgements are not only cruel, it is an \'cfnsanity in itself!!

The best settings for the rehabilitation of the mentally ill is areas in nature of PEACE. There is a real critical need for them to feel safe and secure. For the allowance of stability healing to begin. Combined with the aforementioned good diet, lots of vitamins, with of course NIACIN at the forefront. The higher the dose, the better allowance for individual "Time frames" for it to kick into the system. With these vulnerable souls many are allegorically; flowers, violins and birds. Much nobility and raw courage can be drawn out of these spirits of tight rope tension. Yes, a much needed well of blessed gifts in a desert of a world. No one I know doesn't appreciate a drop of dew on their forehead when burning up with a fever. We would all profit from the "Prophets" among us unsung heroes of the ragged edge. This is the paradox, the resurrection from the crucifixion. The positive emerging from the dungeons of the negative. What can the outcast offer? I tell you MUCH. Vast wisdom can be found in the most "cloaked" coverings. For instance there was this lady that might be around sixty five or so that used to come to the thrift store, I previously talked about. She was in a "worldly label" quite insane. The lipstick she put on was applied all over the border of her lips. She wore wildly coordinated clothing, but held ladies gloves graciously in her hands. She was always buying stuff and would talk about each item she picked up with and old fashioned poetic description. Such previous simplicity of ordinary items. She talked about nature and little adventures of the day. This a big part; the store of her own private world, but she among others has oftentimes profound things to express.

CONCLUSION
WITH AUTHOR'S POEMS

RAW COURAGE SAYS IT ALL

ALL ALONE
I USED TO FEEL ALL ALONE
THEY SAY BEING YOUNG YOU'VE GOT IT MADE
YET WHEN YOU'RE DIFFERENT THE SAME RULES
JUST AREN'T LAID

I'VE LEARNED NOT TO QUESTION
BUT THEN HOW I DID
REJECTION, ATTACKS SEEMED ATTACHED TO MY GRID.

FATE OF AN ILLNESS STRUCK ME BEFORE THIS
CHILD PREDESTINED COULD ENTER THE WORLD
ISOLATION, PAIN BEYOND DEPTHS
GRAVEN SOULS WALKING THE HALLS
SUFFERING SOULS TRAPPED INSIDE WALKING THE
HALLS

YES, I WAS ONE OF THOSE SOULS WALKING THE
HALLS...
GETTING THIS FAR ON A MOUNTAIN IS ONLY FROM
LYING IN A VALLEY...

DESERTS ARE SEEN OH SO DIFFERENT WHEN RARE
RAINS DESCEND
IF TELL YOU MY FRIEND TRULY THE TRIALS DO END

THEME PART

I'LL TELL YOU LIVES ARE JUST RAW COURGE TO
SOME MORE THAN OTHERS
ALL I CAN SEE SOMETIMES IS THE "CORE" THAT ALL
MEN ARE BROTHERS

WHAT DO WE REALLY WANT?
WHAT DO WE REALLY NEED?
A SMILE AT A DESPERATE MOMENT
AN ARM WHEN OUR HEART COULD BLEED
OH RAW COURAGE SAYS IT ALL!!

THIS IS THE SONG OF THE FAITHFUL SOULS
DON'T GIVE UP!
I THOUGHT THAT MYSELF
DON'T PUT THAT VISION UP ON THE SHELF!
WE'RE NOT ALONE
NO! NOT ALONE!
FOR WHEN WE DO WHAT WE'RE MADE FOR
WE FEEL WE'VE COME HOME..

COURAGE TO WALK ON
COURAGE TO THE BEYOND
RAW WHEN THE FINGERS HAVE HELD ON SO
LONG...

WHICH FLOOR ARE YOU ON?

IF WE TALK TO OURSELVES
THE BIG SHOTS SAY WE'RE BANANAS
WE'RE SUPPOSED TO SHUFFLE OFF TO BUFFALO
IN OUR INSTITUTIONAL SLIPPERS AND PAJAMAS
OH THEY ARE SO PROFESSIONAL
MEDICAL WIZARDS OF MENTAL ILLNESS

THAT THERAPY CONSISTS OF LETHARGY
WITH T.V. AND DRUG INDUCED STILLNESS

MORNING CALL OF BREAKFAST
STYROFOAM LUNCH AND DINNER
THE ONE TO ZOMBIE TO ALL THREE
IS THE EVENING T.V. WINNER!

SUPERIOR MINDS ARE KEPT INSIDE
TORMENTED FROM A WAR
A WAR MANKIND IS EVER IN

WHERE DOES THIS ALL LEAVE OFF?
WHERE DOES THIS ALL BEGIN?
WE KNOW WHAT'S REALLY GOING ON
JUST AS WE HAVE ALWAYS KNOWN

BUT WE'RE SHUT UP
FROM REVEALING SUCH
FOR THEIR COVER WOULD BE BLOWN!

GREEN JELLO WAS THE LATEST RAGE
THE 3RD FLOOR'S GOT IT MADE!

THEY HAVE A PSYCH-NURSE NOW THAT DOESN'T
NUDGE
TO PUSH PSYCHOLOGY DOWN THEIR THROATS
WHILE CRAZY KYLE WINCES WITH A SMILE
HE SAYS THEY'LL BE A FLOOD
SO HE'S MAKING BOATS

BOATS OF COLORED PAPER
THEY THINK HE'S WASTING HIS TIME
BUT LITTLE DO THEY KNOW
WHEN THE TRUMPET BLOWS
THEIR THE ONES WHO'VE LOST THEIR MIND!

MAYBE IN A NIGHTMARISH SCENE
AN EXCERPT FROM THE TWILIGHT ZONE
THE PATIENTS WILL BE BEHIND THE COUNTER
AND THE SHRINKS WILL GET A DAY PASS HOME!

WALKING INTO THE RAINBOW

I'VE HAD A SPLINTER IN MY MIND,
SLOWLY TRYING TO MAKE ME MAD

TO BELIEVE IN A BRIGHTER FUTURE
IS MY HOPE FROM THE EGYPT THAT I'VE HAD
YES TO BELIEVE IN A BRIGHTER FUTURE
FROM THE EGYPT THAT I'VE HAD

ONE SUMMER NIGHT I WALKED IN DEEP THOUGHT
TO A GRASS HILL I KNOW

I FELT THE MANTLE OF NOAH
WALKING INTO THE RAINBOW

PASSING THROUGH THE FIRE
ASCENDING FROM THE FLOOD
SLICING WITH THE SWORD
PLEADING WITH THE BLOOD

ANOTHER SUMMER NIGHT I'LL CLIMB TO THAT
GRASSY HILL I KNOW,
I'LL SEE THAT DOVE WITH THE LEAF IN HER MOUTH
AND WALK INTO MY RAINBOW

I'VE LOST THAT SPLINTER IN MY MIND...

THE SEVENTH SIGN

FROM HALLWAYS IN MANSIONS OF HEAVEN
SPEAKS "THE VOICE" AND BREATHES

THE GUFF

SOULS OF ENDLESS FASCINATION CAN NEVER
HAVE ENOUGH
A HEBREW LEGEND SAYS THAT THEY ARE SOULS
AWAITING BIRTH
THE SOULS WITHIN "THE GUFF" TO COME WITHING
A CHILD ON EARTH

SO AS YOU AWAKEN TO A CRISP AND FRAGRANT
MORN'
TO HEAR A SPARROW SING...YOU KNOW AN
INFANT SHALL BE BORN!

WITH PAST AND PRESENT REALMS COMPUTERS
THAT ENTWINE
WITH PROPHECY AND THE SUBLIMINAL..
YOU RECEIVE THE "SEVENTH SIGN"

TECHNOLOGY, DIVINITY

A RAVEN SOARS ABOVE
WITH A JEWISH SYNAGOGUE DESCENDS, THE
CATHOLIC DOVE

THE FUSION OF THE WORLDS INTERSPERSING
THROUGH THE DAY
THE DREAMING OF THE NIGHT
TO WARNINGS OF THE DAY
WARNINGS I OBEY

THE TELEVISION SPLASHES "HIS" MESSAGE ON
THE SCREEN
I THEN PICK UP THE PAPER CONFIRMATIONS THAT
I'VE SEEN

SOME MAY SAY IT'S TOO RIDICULOUS
TOO FOOLISH, TOO SUBLIME
BUT ALL I KNOW ARE THE RESULTS
I'VE RECEIVED THE SEVENTH SIGN.

SO IF YOU SEE A STORM A BREWING AND WINDS
TOO STRONG TO ENDURE
YOU'D BETTER WATCH "THE SEVENTH SIGN"
STARRING DEMI MOORE.....

MANIC PERSUASION

WHEN I SUFFER FROM THIS CONTINUOUS TORMENT
I'M IN A PRISON CELL
NOT A LIVING ROOM

I WOULD LIKE TO HANG MYSELF ON THE NEAREST
BRANCH OF CHERRY TREES
STANDING NOW IN FULL BLOOM

THIS WONDERFUL SECRET LIFE AND MOVEMENT
TROUBLES ME UNSPEAKABLY

THESE ETERNAL BLUE SKIES
THESE COAXING BREEZES
IMPREGNATED WITH SPRING OR AUTUMN MISTS

OH...THEY MAKE ME FRANTIC...
OH...THEY MAKE ME BEWILDERED
AND I ONLY LIKE THE HUMBLEST GRASS OF THE
FIELD
THE STRICKEN DEER
CAN RISE TO THE OCCASION
OR SHRIVEL IN TEARS.

CAN I TAKE "MANIC PERSUASION"
ALTER MY PERCEPTIONS AND SEE THIS ROOM AS
ONE OF MY
ANTIQUE COLLECTIONS?
THIS WONDERFUL SECRET LIFE TROUBLES ME..
BUT I'M TAKING OFF MY CLOAK AND HANGING IT
ON NEAREST CHERRY TREE...

I of course came to write this from our own pain and to help others themselves or loved ones dealing with one of the most misunderstood and incorrectly treated illnesses in the world of medicine itself and of course psychiatry.

May you be encouraged by this autobiography, this scientific, combination with factors you may need to know. For perhaps you or someone dear to you is exhibiting signs of mental illness, then you will be better armed to get them onto a program quickly, before the ravages of the illness, or worse yet the damage, of the psychiatric realm. Getting their ignorant hands on that person, better yet YOU AND GOD GET YOUR HANDS ON THAT PERSON. With what I've painstakingly written here, this is the blue print the reference, some of you will desperately need to refer to. I write this not to my fame, but for the rescuing of those so neglected and miserably treated. This will not continue. Be part of this REVOLUTION TO RESCUE. It is not a greater sin of those who did nothing, but of those who knew what to do and did nothing. I MYSELF AM GUILTY OF NOT GETTING THIS BOOK PUBLISHED SOONED AND TO THE MANY SOULS THAT HAVE NOT BEEN RESCUED AND TO THEIR FAMILIES, I PROMISE I WILL DO ALL IN MY POWER TO MAKE A BIG DIFFERENCE NOW.

IN HIS HOLY HONOUR.

TO THE FATHER WHO IS THE FATHER OF US ALL.

AGAIN, NOW SADLY I GIVE CREDIT AND LOVE TO THE

LATE DR. HOFFER.

DR. HOFFER, YOU POINTED US ULTIMATELY TO GOD AND BECAUSE OF YOU, I AM NOW MORE

HEALTHY AND RADIANT THAN MOST. THOUGH EVEN WELL, LIFE HAS STILL BEEN VERY HARD. BUT MY COPING SKILLS AND CHISELED CHARACTER HAVE BEEN "HONED" TO LIVE LIFE DEEPLY, TO HELP OTHERS LESS FORTUNATE. ABOVE ALL MY FAITH HAS DEFINITELY PULLED ME HIGHER WHEN THIS BODY HAS BEEN TOO WEAK TO FIGHT.

—Lou anne Metcalfe

CPSIA information can be obtained at www.ICGtesting.com
Printed in the USA
LVOW040758210912

299647LV00001B/47/P